Hunters' Guide
To Professional Outfitters
1988

Hunters' Guide
To Professional Outfitters Worldwide 1988 Edition

STONE HOUSE PUBLISHING INC.

PUBLISHED ANNUALLY BY:
STONE HOUSE PUBLISHNG INC.
25 MacDonald Avenue
Dartmouth, Nova Scotia
Canada B3B 1C6

Canadian Cataloguing in Publication Data
Main entry under title:
Hunters' Guide to Professional Outfitters

1988 ed., 1st
Includes index.
ISBN 0-921128-00-2

1. Big game hunting - Equipment and supplies -
Directories. 2. Safaris - Equipment and supplies -
Directories. 3. Hunting - Equipment and supplies -
Directories.

SK273.H86 1988   688.7'92'0294   C87-095017-7

Design: Arthur Carter, Carter Communication
Production: Stephen Ewins and Arthur Carter
Advertising: Sherman Hines, Gillian Manchester,
        Debbie Bellefontaine and Chris Jones
Statistics: Gillian Manchester
Publisher: Sherman Hines
General Manager: Dan Sargeant

DISTRIBUTION:

Africa and Europe:
Russell Friedman Books (Pty) Ltd.
P.O. Box 73
Halfway House 1685
South Africa
Telephone (011) 702-2300/1
Telex: 4-28133

United States
Stackpole Books
P.O. Box 1831, Cameron & Kelker Sts.,
Harrisburg, PA 17105
Telephone (717) 234-5041

Canada
Servidec, 50 Main Street,
Ottawa, Ontario K1S 1B2
Telephone (613) 237-5577

Printed and Bound in Hong Kong
ISBN 0-91128-00-2
ISSN 0835-8648

Front Cover Photo:
Trophy Room, Lynn and
Penny Castle, Wood River
Lodge, Alaska
Photo: Sherman Hines

Front Cover Inset Photo:
Arctic Adventures,
Outfitters
Photo: Sherman Hines

Endpapers Engraving from:
Holland & Holland

HOW TO USE THIS BOOK

The Hunters' Guide to Professional Outfitters is your primary source of information you can use to plan your next major hunting or fishing trip.

Begin with the Table of Contents to determine, first of all, your geographic preference. Whether it's Africa or America, this book offers full page advertisements from some of the world's finest outfitters. Then, once you've found the type of hunting or fishing you desire, in the location of your liking, turn to the sections on booking agents, supplies, taxidermists and so on to find those additional services necessary to make your hunt complete.

In the Directory section in the the back of the book you will find a complete listing from around the world. Once again, these are grouped geographically so that you can plan your travel as easily as possible.

For more detailed information on any of the advertisers or directory entrants, just clip and fill out a reader service card from the page at the back of the book and mail it to the outfitter/supplier of your choice.

Remember, this book is an annual publication. Each year it will grow to include more and more services catering to hunters and fishermen. As it does, it will become even more useful to you. You can obtain each year's edition by contacting the publisher for direct mail order, through a bookstore for retail purchase; or, drop by our booth at some of the major hunting shows and exhibitions.

Outfitters and Suppliers:

If you would like to advertise in this book or have your name added to the Directory, we'd be pleased to hear from you. Contact Stone House Publishing and we'll provide you with all the information you need.

STONE HOUSE PUBLISHNG INC.
25 MacDonald Avenue
Dartmouth, Nova Scotia
Canada B3B 1C6

Sections

Contents

1   *Big Game Outfitters*

North America

2   *Fishing Outfitters*

3   *Booking Agents*

4   *Rifles and Accessories*

5   *Optics and Scopes*

6   *Ammunition and Accessories*

7   *Supplies*

8   *Taxidermists*

9   *Artists*

10   *Airlines and Travel*

11   *Outfitters Directory*

You are holding in your hands the first annual *Hunters Guide to Professional Outfitters.*

It is the world's only up-to-date annual reference book for hunters listing professional outfitters, taxidermists, booking agents, suppliers, rifles, scopes, ammunition, artists and transportation. A must for the up-to-date hunter, who needs current information about the hunting industry.

On every page you will find the quality of information that will save you hours and even days of research to find these suppliers. This book will allow you to sit down in the comfort of your den or trophy room and find the outfitters and suppliers for your next trip. This annual will also serve as a research source over the years as a pictorial record of the trophies taken consistently by outfitters around the world.

Sherman Hines

Sherman Hines
publisher

WHAT IT MEANS TO BE A PROFESSIONAL HUNTER

A professional hunter is first and foremost a people person who uses his skill and knowledge of the wilderness in such a way that others may benefit from it. He is the catalyst who enables the client to obtain his trophy, in such a manner which is enjoyable and fulfilling, and within the physical prowess of the hunter. His profound respect and love of the wilderness and the game it produces are important to his client at all times. The hunt and the actual kill are just a facet of the overall experience. The achievement of this is the most rewarding when one sees the understanding and appreciation of nature begin to register in the eyes of the person you are guiding, whether young or old. Friendships are forged in the furnace of nature, and cut across social, financial and cultural barriers to the very heart of things.

From such experiences, Theodore Roosevelt's guide Frederick Selous, who guided him in Africa just after the turn of the century, became his greatest friend. Men from different countries, different backgrounds, whose languages were different ended up with genuine friendships. We, the Professional Hunters, have all experienced these friendships which would not have been possible without the common denominator, of nature, stripping us down to our true selves when we face her in the raw. When you share danger, joy, appetite and hunger, weather, sunrise and sunset, the disappointments, the wet, the cold, the trophy at your feet, experiencing the fulfilment of nature with another person; then you know one another. Friendships are born of this knowledge which would not have been

as good conservationalists, may we perpetuate it into the future so that our sons may say one day, "Dad was a Professional Hunter. He conserved for tomorrow, he hunted ethically, guided his clients at the level of the client's physical ability, not his own, and he has friends all over the world who welcome him in their homes, because he made them feel at home in his — the great outdoors."

Don Lindsay
President
International Professional
Hunters Association

Game Big
Outfitters Outfitters
Game Big Game
fitters Outfitters
Big Game Big Ga
Outfitters Outfit
Game Big Game
fitters Outfitters
Game Bi
Big Game Ou

Big Game Outfitters

Big Game
Outfitters
Big Game
Outfitters
Big Game
Outfitters
Outfitters
Big Game
Game Big
Outfitters Outfitte
Big Game
Game Big Game
fitters Outfitters
Outfitters 1 0

KEITH N. JOHNSON
WILDMAN LAKE LODGE • ALASKA
Guiding & Outfitting for Alaska Big Game over 20 years

3646 North Point Drive, Anchorage, Alaska 99515
Phone (907) 243-5087

ONE OF THE FINEST BUSH LODGE ACCOMMODATIONS AVAILABLE IN ALASKA
Wildman Lake Lodge is able to accommodate our individual hunts as well as group hunts of up to twelve people. With outlying permanent cabins, tent frames, and tent camps we can effectively utilize the finest big game hunting area in Alaska. The lodge itself includes two bunk rooms, two private rooms, shower and dining facilities, as well as two private cabins and a guide's cabin. Just a few steps from the lodge door, you will find outstanding fishing for rainbow trout, arctic char, salmon and dolly varden, as well as excellent bird hunting for duck, geese and ptarmigan.

MASTER GUIDE OUTFITTER
Licensed from the Yukon River to the Peninsula
Member: Alaska Professional Hunters Association, Foundation for North American Wild Sheep, National Rifle Association, Safari International

Fly-In Hunting & Fishing On the Alaskan Peninsula at WILDMAN LAKE LODGE
Permanent & Tent Frame Cabins
Tent Camps — Back Pack Hunts

Individual & Combination Species Hunts On the Alaskan Peninsula
— May, September & October —
Caribou • Brown Bear • Moose Wolf and Wolverine
Quality Bird Hunting for Duck, Geese & Ptarmigan
Fishing for Rainbow, Arctic Char, Salmon & Dolly Varden

CHUCK WIRSCHEM
ALASKAN GUIDE AND OUTFITTER

NICE BROOKS RANGE RAM
FLOAT-FISHING / 9 SPECIES

We specialize in high quality experiences hunting: Dall Rams, Brown Bear and float fishing. I've been adventuring in Alaska for 24 years. The last 14 years I've had 100% success on all sheep hunts. All hunts are guided one on one. My son and I will give you quality personalized attention. I have large exclusive guide areas to insure a high success ratio.

BROOKS RANGE BASE CAMP
BROWN BEAR CAMP, ALASKA PENINSULA

FIRST DAY SUCCESS!

CHUCK WIRSCHEM, 6608 BLACKBERRY, ANCHORAGE, ALASKA 99502 907-243-1649

Multiple Use Managers guides are well experienced, most of them are wildlife biologists as well. Wayne Long, owner / biologist / guide has over 25 years experience in managing wildlife and hunting operations.

MULTIPLE USE MANAGERS, INC.

P.O. Box L
West Point, CA 95255
(209) 293-7087

Specialists in:
Planning
Developing
and Managing
of Recreation
and Wildlife
Resources

MULTIPLE USE MANAGERS INC.
QUALITY HUNTING AT QUALITY LOCATIONS

At our 54,000 acre SANTA ROSA ISLAND off the coast of Southern California, we have the world's best trophy Roosevelt Elk hunting as well as excellent mule deer hunting. In Northern California on our 63,000 acre DYE CREEK PRESERVE we offer outstanding hunting for black-tailed deer, wild boar, upland game and waterfowl; also fishing for bass, trout and steelhead. Trophy class Columbian Black-tailed Deer are available at our north coast PILOT ROCK DEER CLUB. We also provide exceptionally good HONKER and DUCK hunting on two different properties in Southern Oregon.

46" Dall Sheep shot in Canada's Yukon Territory

HUNT CANADA'S
YUKON

Dall, Stone and Fannin Sheep • Moose • Mountain Caribou • Barren Ground Caribou
Goat • Grizzly • Black Bear • Wolf • Wolverine

The Yukon Outfitters' Association

Melvin Spohn shot this huge **world record** Alaska-Yukon moose in Canada's Yukon Territory. Its antlers measured 73 1/8 inches across the widest spread. The current edition of the **SCI Record Book of Trophy Animals** scores it at 297 5/8 points, the new record for the species.

The Yukon Outfitters' Association is a group of dedicated registered big game outfitters. Together, their hunting areas cover roughly 185,000 square miles of rugged unspoiled wilderness. The area has some of the finest hunting and fishing, as well as scenic beauty, left in the world today.

All of us are dedicated to the conservation and management of our wildlife resources. The Yukon Outfitters' Association works very closely with the Yukon Game Branch. Our objective is better quality service for the **non** resident hunter and sportsman. Yukon Outfitters' Association members are substantial contributors to the Foundation for North American Wild Sheep, Safari Club International and Wildlife Management Projects of the Yukon Government, and the Department of Tourism, Yukon.

YUKON OUTFITTERS ASSOCIATION

YUKON OUTFITTERS ASSOCIATION

RICK FURNISS
Yukon Outfitting
Hunt Consultant & Professional Hunter
Box 5364, Whitehorse, Yukon, Canada Y1A 4Z2
403-667-2712

INTRODUCTION: The Yukon Territory is a 207,000 square mile huge undeveloped mountain country with only 22,000 residents, 16,000 of which live in the capital of Whitehorse. This territory is literally the last frontier, especially for hunting. My hunting area is over 10,000 square miles making it one of the largest hunting concessions in the world. By comparison, my hunting area is much larger than Switzerland and is over three times the size of Yellowstone park, the largest game sanctuary in the continental USA. I have the exclusive rights to outfit hunters in this vast area, much of which has never been hunted.

I offer hunts by horse packtrain, rubber raft river float and fly-in backpacking for all ages and physical abilities. I hunt the area lightly and usually hunt new country with each party by moving base camps. To do this we hunt primarily from mobile tent camps in the manner traditional to the North. My hunts are an adventure and an experience, as well as hunting expeditions I provide comfortable camps and good food but there is no luxury. I take a limited number of clients to assure a high quality personalized service.

I've hunted all 27 North American big game. I'm an archer and official scorer for Pope & Young archery records. I have experience flying the bush. Outfitting has been my full time profession since 1975. Licenced as guide since 1967. I am an active member of Yukon Outfitters Association, Int'l. Professional Hunters Association (currently vice-president) and Safari Club Int'l. I am a Canadian and a permanent Yukon resident.

NANCY and RICK FURNISS

HUNT THE CANADIAN YUKON

RICK FURNISS

Yukon Outfitting

Hunt Consultant & Professional Hunter
Box 5364, Whitehorse, Yukon, Canada Y1A 4Z2
403-667-2712

TROPHY CARIBOU

We have some of the best central barren-ground caribou hunting in Canada. We offer three hunting locations in eastern, central, and western Arctic. We hunt on Foxe Peninsula on Baffin Island, on Melville Peninsula, on north-west shore of Hudson Bay, and in the Coppermine Highlands in Northwest Territories mainland. A 7 day 2x1 hunt costs $2,485 U.S. The special package price includes roundtrip airfare from Ottawa, Winnipeg or Edmonton. Second caribou $500 U.S.
For more information contact:

Canada North Outfitting Inc.,
P.O. Box 1230,
Waterdown, Ontario
Canada L0R 2H0
Tel: (416) 689-7925
Telex No.: 061 8996 CNO WTDN

CANADA NORTH OUTFITTING INC.   416 689-7925

Muskox

Of over 200 muskox trophy hunters the past 6 years, all but 2 have been successful. Many muskox taken are over 100 points, while the #1 in the Safari Club International book comes in at over 120 points. Look at the record book to see the number of trophies in the top 10 taken by our clients!

Hunts take place in October and early November as well as late February, March and April.

Polar Bear

One of the most exciting and traditional hunts in the world, the Polar Bear hunt, covers 15 days. Although the Polar Bear cannot be exported to the U.S.A., there are now upwards of 50 Polar Bear trophy hunts annually in the Northwest Territories — the only area in the world to hunt Polar Bear.

Peary Caribou

"Peary Caribou" have only been sports hunted since 1983, and although smaller than our "Canadian Central Barren-Ground Caribou," are a unique species and listed in the "Safari Club" record book. Season for trophies is between October 10th and November 10th.

Peary Caribou are a unique Canadian sub-species, found only on the Arctic Islands. Inuit (Eskimo) hunters have primarily left large adult male caribou alone if favour of the more tender meat of females and the young.

Arctic Hunts

Since 1977 Qaivvik has offered Polar Bear, Muskox and, more recently, Peary Caribou and combination trophy hunts to the discerning sportsman.

These have been offered in a number of Arctic communities now including Holman, Melville Island, Eskimo Point, Repulse Bay, Sachs Harbour, Paulatuk and Cambridge Bay.

The Inuit (Eskimo) do all of the guiding by dogteam for Polar Bear and by snowmachine for Muskox and Peary Caribou. All Arctic hunts are in the winter months; October and November, and February through April. All gear, including tents, food and sleeping bags, as well as the trophy hunter, are transported by Komotik (or sled) pulled by the dog team or snow machine.

Caribou or down clothing and Arctic sleeping bags are provided by Qaivvik, while a detailed information kit is forwarded to all confirmed hunters.

HUNT THE CANADIAN ARCTIC

Fred A. Webb and Sons • Professional Hunters
R.R. #1, Nictau, Plaster Rock
New Brunswick, Canada E0J 1W0 (506) 356-8312
U.S. ADDRESS: WEBB-QAIVVIK LTD., 441 CHURCH RD., LANDSDALE, PA. 19446 (215) 362-1510

Nictau, New Brunswick, Canada

Dear Sportsman,

Thank you for inquiring about our trips to the Canadian Northland. We have a long tradition in the hunting business. From the days of the month-long trip in the eastern wilderness for moose and caribou, until the present, when jet travel allows 10-day trips to the high arctic, members of our family have been guiding big game hunters.

It is a Canada-wide operation, working as we do at various seasons from Newfoundland to the Yukon. Fred Webb, of the present generation, began guiding bear and deer hunters in New Brunswick in the early fifties. In the late fifties he began working in the north, first as a guide and communications specialist on scientific exploration parties, and later in the development of big game hunts and fishing trips with the natives of the area. Two sons, Martin and Derek, are rapidly catching up as they expand their expertise in various aspects of the operation.

We term ourselves "Professional Hunters," rather than outfitters or booking agents, as our operation goes beyond the scope of either profession. In some cases we own the real estate and operate as outfitters. On other hunts we are partners, working primarily with the native Inuit (Eskimo), and Dene (Indian) peoples, developing, consulting, operating and booking the finest hunts available for all the northern species.

This is a year-round, full-time profession. With our years of experience and the cooperation of other top people in the business, we assure you a safe, enjoyable, and highly successful hunting experience.

Sincerely,

Fred

Fred A. Webb

Quebec

We are pleased to work with the Inuit (Eskimo) people of Ungava Bay in extreme northern Quebec, operating the only camps actually located on the bay itself. There we hunt the George River Quebec-Labrador caribou herd, currently about 650,000 animals. Caribou in the hunt area are semi-resident and not subject to dramatic population swings; they spend the entire

hunting season right on the coast. Since opening the first camp in 1981, trophy hunts have been 100% successful and resulted in a large number of record book entries.

Inuit guides are trained in proper field caping and in-camp taxidermists prepare the head for later shipment and mounting. Official scorers are in camp. Two animals per license; hunts are late August and September.

Northwest Territories and the Yukon

Fred Webb and Sons now have an interst in Qaivvik, Ltd., operating out of Yellowknife, Northwest Territories. Over the years Qaivvik (pronounced Kyevik) has hosted hundreds of hunters from all over the world, working with a number of Inuit communities to hunt central Canada barren ground caribou (now recognized as a separate Boone and Crockett big game trophy category), muskox, polar bear and Peary caribou.

To hunt central Canada barren ground caribou, hunters are flown to the main base camp at Courageous Lake, 150 miles northeast of Yellowknife. This camp, located above the tree-line, consists of guest tents, a cook/dining tent, staff tents and shower. In fall, the 350,000 strong Bathurst herd migrates south, spread out over many miles of the barrens. Usually they can be hunted successfully right from the lake, but flyouts are arranged to spike camps, as required. Wolf and wolverine may also be taken as animals of opportunity on this hunt; a small fee is charged.

In addition, grizzly bear and Dall sheep hunts can be arranged in Northwest Territories or the Yukon.

Webb-Qaivvik offers arctic hunts for polar bear, muskox and Peary caribou, singly or in combination, from various far northern communities. Inuit do all the guiding for polar bear by use of dogteam, and by snow machine for muskox and Peary caribou. These hunts are conducted during the months of October and November, and February through April. All equipment and the hunter are transported by machine- or dog-pulled sled. For these hunts, caribou or down clothing and arctic sleeping bags are supplied by Webb-Qaivvik, and a detailed information kit is sent to all booked hunters.

The traditional polar bear hunt lasts up to 15 days, and is affected most by climatic conditions and the abundance of seal, the bear's primary food source. Trophies to 10½ feet have been taken by several hunters. The small, white Peary caribou is found only on certain arctic islands and is now included in Safari Club's North American big game records book. Hunts are from mid-October to mid-November. Muskox make a unique and impressive trophy; we have virtually 100% success and have placed numerous animals in the record book. Hunts take place both spring and fall.

TRAVEL TO CANADA'S NORTHLAND

NOUVEAU • QUEBEC
Land of Arctic Adventures

COME LIVE YOUR DREAM

The Land of Arctic Adventures

Arctic Quebec is a different world from the one we know. It's a world of treeless tundra ridges, of brawling rivers where trout and salmon abound, a world diamond studded with literally thousands of lakes many of which have yet to feel the dip of a paddle or the splash of a lure.

For eight months of the year this world is locked under ice and snow, but when summer comes the pace of life is intense. On the calving grounds young caribou test their legs, somehow sensing that every second counts before the October snows again sweep the land. On the tundra ponds Canada geese guard over goslings which within months will embark on an epic journey to the southern wintering grounds. And among the tag alders in sheltered gulleys, ptarmigan call raucously to each other.

For sportsman and nature lover, outdoor enthusiast and photographer, Arctic Quebec is a new world to discover. It's a sportsman's paradise.

IN THE LAND OF THE INUIT

. . . and you'll find a lifetime of memories in the land of the Inuit.

Quebec's tundra region is a vast land of rolling tundra ridges and brawling rivers, a land still young and unfettered, where you can find clear horizons and solitude. Its southern boundary is the taiga located some 600 miles north of New York City, to the west are the steely waters of Hudson Bay, to the east the cold waters of the Labrador Sea which stretches north like a giant horseshoe around Ungava Bay. In all, this land of the Inuit covers some 300,000 square miles.

This is the land of the Inuit. A total of 6,000 Inuit and a smattering of whites from the south call Arctic Quebec home. While many reside in Kuujjuaq (Fort Chimo, population 1,150), most live in scattered settlements along the shores of Ungava and Hudson Bay, clinging to the ways of their forefathers and at the same time adapting to the innovations from the south.

Their culture dates back some 4,000 years and they've adapted well to the rigors of their environment. It's a way of life basically dependant on fishing and hunting for subsistence and, while the Inuit have adopted many of white man's inventions, they retain an inbred ability to understand the ways of the animals with which they share this vastness; an ability to comprehend the migration habits of the fish, the animals and birds and predict their patterns.

For this also is the land of the caribou. Numbering some 600,000 head, they roam free and wild across the tundra ridges, forever following the restless winds — great herds that wander through the seasons.

Here, in this land of the Inuit, is where memories are made, where adventure lingers.

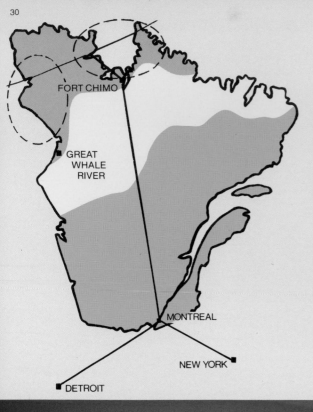

One of the foremost Atlantic
world famous George River -
in the tundra to flow into Ung
rivers have runs of strong, se
weighing 20 pounds or more
and hefty lakers are found a
At our caribou camps hunter
dozen record book racks eve

Yet this arctic region is far m
you can experience another
opportunity to become, for a
a part of this land of the Inui

Your Lodgin

In the settlements, comforta
for visitors in either private h
in hotels. Away from the sett
At established fishing camps
comfortable, complete with
even a smokehouse. The car
necessity, somewhat more S
tent cabins which sleep two
comes equipped with a heat
of the cooler nights. The out
necessity, consist of one or

All photos by © **SHERMAN HINES**

Your Hosts

Descended from the Thule Culture which thrived in the western Arctic some 2,000 years before Christ, the Inuit of Arctic Quebec are a unique and friendly people. While they maintain their language and customs as best they can in today's fast changing world, most do have an ability to converse in English. They welcome you to share their way of life and they'll go out of their way to explain their traditions and history.

Both guides and camp staff are largely Inuit families from nearby settlements. All are helpful and the kitchen staff is up before anybody else to prepare fresh-baked bread and pies. You instantly feel you've become one of the family and it's always difficult to leave — only a resolve to return again makes the parting easier.

rivers — the
s its strength deep
Most of the other
ctic char often
t brook trout
erywhere.
etter than three
n.

s a land where
fe. It's an
ment in time,

ngs are arranged
when available,
conditions vary.
ommodations are
er showers and
ps are, by
— consisting of
isitors. Each
the chill out
ps, by
as tents.

For Your Safety

With more than three decades of experience behind us, Arctic Adventures looks after every detail to ensure that you have a safe and worry-free adventure in the land of the Inuit. We can boast a history of safety and service, thanks to our knowledge of the north and our network of co-ops throughout Arctic Quebec.

Our boats are sturdy and safe 24-foot freighter canoes powered by 25 horsepower outboard motors and equipped with life preservers. Each camp is equipped with radio communications in case of an emergency.

From the time you book one of our Arctic adventures, you can relax, knowing that all details will be looked after every step of the way, thanks to the diligence of our coordinators in Montreal, Kuujjuaq (Fort Chimo) and at camp.

As the biggest and most experienced organization in Arctic Quebec, we've taken advantage of modern technology — jet travel, satelite communications and portable power plants to ensure that you have a memorable Arctic adventure.

In 1959 la Fédération des Coopératives du Nouveau–Quebec, an organization which unites the Inuit co-ops of Canada's eastern Arctic, was created and part of its mandate was to develop the tourism potential of Arctic Quebec. To accomplish this the Federation created Arctic Adventures which, more than three decades later, has brought literally thousands of visitors from the south to live in the land of the Inuit. It's an experience few can forget and all dream of reliving.

Transportation

Not so long ago, Arctic Quebec was inaccessible to all but a select few. Today, modern jets whisk visitors comfortably from Montreal to Kuujjuaq (Fort Chimo), gateway to the eastern tundra. On the tarmack, a modern twin-engine Otter awaits to take you on the last leg of your journey to native settlements along the shores of Ungava or Hudson Bay, or inland to one of several tundra camps for your Arctic Adventure.

ARCTIC ADVENTURES

8102 Trans Canada Highway
Ville St. Laurent
Montreal, Quebec, Canada H4S 1R4
Phone (514) 332-0880

EXPER

the adventure o

CHOLLY SMITH • OUTFITTERS
SILVER RANCH
OUTFITTERS
B.C. CANADA
651•7515

RIENCE

untamed lands

Are you planning an outdoor holiday? An incomparable experience awaits you at Indian River Ranch in beautiful northern British Columbia. Here, you can collect memories to last a lifetime. Ringed by a glacial crescent which emanates from the Juneau Alaska Icefield, this area of lakes, rivers, mountains and forests affords the vacationer a variety of holiday experiences from peaceful and relaxing to adventurous and stimulating.

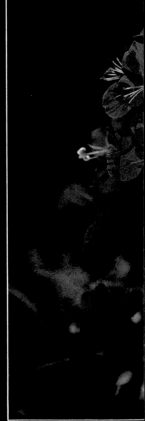

Capture the romance of the gold rush era.

Visit the site of the original gold claim that in 1898 became the Town of Discovery near Atlin B.C. Pan for gold and experience the thrill of discovering gold dust in your pan. Visit Whitehorse. Tour the museum and the restored paddlewheeler. Shop for soapstone sculpture, furs and Inuit arts and crafts.

Marvel at the Beauty of nature

Hundreds of species of flowers and plants are to be found in this area. Learn about the edible plants and berries of the north.

Enjoy the scenic rivers and lakes

With hundreds of rivers and thousands of lakes in the 4000 square mile area, there is unlimited opportunity to experience the beauties of nature. Hike, travel by pack horse or canoe.

Ride through forests and over mountains

The peace and quiet of the countryside will be yours. Thrill to being in the wilderness under the care and guidance of the experienced staff from Indian River Ranch.

Delight in the wildlife

Moose, caribou, wolf, goat, sheep, grizzly and black bears are all big game found in the area. Duck, Ptarmigan, Canada Geese, hawks and eagles are only a few of the species of birds that live and nest along the trails and at the water's edge.

INTERNATIONAL
PROFESSIONAL HUNTERS' ASSOCIATION

BOX 17444 SAN ANTONIO TEXAS 78217 U S A
TELEPHONE 512/824-7509

PRESIDENT
Don Lindsay

VICE PRESIDENTS
WESTERN SECTOR
Lynn Castle

Rick Furniss

Mike Branham

Dooley Gilchrist

VICE PRESIDENTS
EASTERN/AFRICAN SECTOR
Tony Sanchez Arino

Robin Hurt

Coenraad Vermaak

Terry Pierson

The I.P.H.A. has stringent entry requirements
for its members.

They are subject to the scrutiny of a
disciplinary enquiry in the case of complaint.

Each member pledges:

- TO PROMOTE WORLDWIDE, THE GOOD MANAGEMENT
OF WILDLIFE
- TO COLLABORATE WITH GOVERNMENTS IN THE
CONSERVATION OF FLORA AND FAUNA
- TO MAINTAIN A SPORTSMANLIKE CONCEPT OF
HUNTING
- TO PREVENT ILLEGAL AND UNSPORTSMANLIKE
PRACTICES
- TO SAFEGUARD WORLDWIDE, THE INTERESTS OF
CLIENTS.

This is a worldwide brotherhood of
professionals, with an international clientele.

THE CREAM OF THE PROFESSIONALS

I P H A is at your service. For further
information or assistance please write to
IPHA, P.O. Box 1317, Parklands, 2121, South
Africa.

LAMOUREUX OUTFITTERS LTD.

Martin and Sharon Lamoureux
Gen. Del., Ft. Ware, B.C., Canada V0J 3B0
Radio Mobile: 604-047-121, Ask the Ft. Nelson operator for 2M3827 on Fox Pass Channel.

- STONE SHEEP
- MOUNTAIN GOAT
- GRIZZLY BEAR
- MOOSE
- MOUNTAIN CARIBOU
- BLACK BEAR
- WOLVES AND WOLVERINE

HUNT IN NORTHERN BRITISH COLUMBIA

Trophy hunts in the Sifton/Kechika Range of mountains, management units 7-40 and 7-41. Hunts can be with horses, packstring, backpacking and riverboat, therefore we can arrange a trip to suit almost any person's needs.

We have clean, comfortable camps, with lodges, cabins and tents set in spectacular scenery. There is an abundance of wildlife in our remote wilderness area and each year we take some exceptional trophy animals.

This area is well known for its **Grizzly Bear** and trophy **Mountain Goat**.

SEASONS:

SPRING   Grizzly Bear / Black Bear   12 days

SUMMER   Fishing at its best! Excellent trout, rainbow, dolly varden, arctic char, grayling, northern pike.

River boat trips, camping, fishing, photography for the entire family.

FALL
- 15 day   Stone Sheep / Goat
- 15 day   Grizzly / Moose
- 15 day   Moose / Mountain Goat / Mountain Caribou
- 8 or 7 day   Trophy backpacking Goat hunts
- 10 day   riverboat Moose / Black Bear

.. HUNTING .. FISHING .. PHOTOGRAPHY ..

MOON LAKE

The heart of the Taku Plateau in northwestern British Columbia is an unspoiled, almost untrodden, area of Canada. It is a land of mountains, river valleys and sub-Arctic tundra where Dall and fannin sheep, mountain goals, grizzly and black bears, mountain caribou, moose, wolves and wolverine roam freely with little or no intrusion from the outside world.

Moon Lake Outfitters' hunting area commences on the west shore of Atlin Lake, the largest natural lake in British Columbia. It extends 65 miles west to the Alaska border and north to the Yukon border. It is here that Ed and Janice Smith have built beautiful log cabins on five scenic lakes which provide every hunter-comfort imaginable. Mouth-watering home cooked meals, radio communications, excellent pack and riding horses have all attributed to the Smith's impeccable reputation. Ed is a licensed pilot and uses his own aircraft to service the camps.

Either Ed, who has 12 years guiding experience, or one of his experienced staff will guide hunting and fishing clients amidst 2,500 square miles of breath takingly beautiful mountains.

Bear hunting begins in the early weeks of spring. Sheep and caribou are hunted throughout the summer, with moose added in the fall. Racine, Teakettle, Tutski - meaningless now — will be remembered, long after hunting and fishing these areas, as a 40-inch ram, a 60-inch moose or a 20-pound trout.

Fishing trips are offered from June 1 to August 30. Clients experience the thrill of fishing wilderness lakes, rivers and streams for northern pike, lake trout and Arctic greyling.

Clients are met at the airport in Whitehorse, Yukon and flown directly to base camps near Atlin, British Columbia, a town made famous during the gold rush era at the turn of the century. From here, the type of hunt, the terrain and the distance to be travelled dictate the method of transportation — either by float plane, boat, pack string or hiking.

Ed and Janice Smith
P.O. Box 161
Atlin, B.C., Canada
V0W 1A0   604-651-7515
Yukon Mobile Operator
White Mountain Channel 2M8424

MOONLAKE OUTFITTERS LTD.

Ed and Janice Smith
P.O. Box 161
Atlin, B.C., Canada
V0W 1A0   604-651-7515
Yukon Mobile Operator
White Mountain Channel 2M8424

NOVAS

Nova Scotia's famous "Indian Summer" will stretch the glorious fall hunting season weeks longer than most — but, it's still not long enough . . .

. . . For there are puddle ducks and sea ducks and geese and brant; pheasants and woodcock and partridge and grouse; deer and bear and rabbit and coyote. Never enough time! Never enough vacation!

Make sure you have your time booked early.

Contact any of the outfitters listed below, today. We look forward to hearing from you.

A modern, secluded lodge on an eight acre island providing a full line of services for trout and salmon fishing, and bird, bear and deer hunting.

Call or write for details: Don Breen
P.O. Box 402, Milton, Queens County, Nova Scotia,
B0T 1P0
(902) 354-4354

Accommodation for 4-6 overlooking the magnificent Lake Bras d'Or. One licensed guide for every two people. Hunting for rabbit, waterfowl, upland birds and our specialty — white tail deer. Great fishing for salmon, rainbow, speckled and brown trout.

Contact: Earl Rudderham
RR #2, Boisdale, Christmas Island
Cape Breton, Nova Scotia, B0A 1C0
(902) 871-2549

Comfortable accommodations and experienced guide service for brook and lake trout, bass fishing. Hunting guides for showshoe hare, upland and big game including white tail deer and black bear.

Contact: Robert & Marie Gauthier
RR#2, Annapolis County, Nova Scotia, B0S 1A0
(902) 638-3509

Quality guiding, comfortable lodgings and hearty meals in the middle of some of the finest trout and salmon fishing, and big game hunting anywhere.

Contact: Aubrey R. Beaver
P.O. Box 40, Sherbrooke, Nova Scotia, B0J 3C0
(902) 522-2235

Knowledgeable outfitting services for Atlantic salmon, brown trout, upland birds and big game in one of Nova Scotia's most outstanding lodges.

Contact: Tom & Marion Kennedy
Upper Stewiacke Valley, Nova Scotia, B0N 2P0
(902) 671-2749

PHOTO BY DAN CALLIS

Single party bookings in each of our two lodges and one guide for every two hunters ensure privacy for hunting upland birds, white tail deer and black bear.

Write or call: Roger & Anna Ehrenfeld
P.O. Box 149, Middleton, Nova Scotia, B0S 1P0
(902) 825-4030 (days) or (902) 825-6629 (evenings)

Salmon and trout fishing in two famous streams, hunting for upland birds, waterfowl and big game from a comfortable, secluded lodge on the Medway River.

Call or write: Moyal Conrad
Greenfield, Queens County, Nova Scotia, B0T 1E0
(902) 685-2423 (lodge) (902) 685-2378/ 2376

Outfitting services for fishing and hunting — smallmouth & striped bass, salmon, ducks, geese and white tail deer in the Annapolis Valley and the South Shore of Nova Scotia.

Please call or write: Ron Seney
Meisner's Section, RR#3, New Germany, Nova Scotia, B0R 1E0 (902) 644-3015

SENTINEL SAFETY CONSULTANTS

Experienced guides, home cooked meals and private hunting land for snowshoe hare, white tail deer, black bear and fishing for Atlantic salmon and brown trout.

Please contact: David & Linda Kennedy
RR#3, Brookfield, Colchester County, Nova Scotia, B0N 1C0
(902) 673-2023

Two secluded cabins on the St. Mary's River providing guides for trout and salmon fishing and white tail deer hunting.

Contact: Phillip Turner
RR#1, Aspen, Guysborough County, Nova Scotia, B0H 1E0
(902) 833-2303

Jack MacIsaac
Minister of Tourism

BEAVER ISLAND LODGE

IN THE WILDERNESS OF WESTERN
NOVA SCOTIA, CANADA

P.O. BOX 402
MILTON, QUEEN'S COUNTY
NOVA SCOTIA, CANADA
B0T 1P0
PHONE: (902) 354-4354

Three professional guides
are available to take our
guests trout fishing in spring
and summer; canoeing on white water
or bird hunting each fall.

Complete privacy and total seclusion
are yours when you visit our modern,
fully-equipped lodge located on an eight-
acre island in a large lake in south western
Nova Scotia. The five-bedroom, two-
storey lodge can accommodate up to ten
guests comfortably.

One of Eastern Canada's finest outfitting enterprises, Lansdowne Lodge combines all the comforts of a modern home, including hearty meals, with high quality guide service for a totally satisfying outdoor vacation.

Each member of staff is a master guide, registered by the Province of Nova Scotia; knowledgeable, courteous, and capable of catering to elderly sportsmen.

THE COMPLEX INCLUDES . . .

- Two modern, attractive buildings located on the banks of the Upper Stewiacke River
- Luxurious interior right down to the deep-pile, fitted carpeting
- Full baths with modern fixtures
- Fully-equipped kitchen
- Telephone
- Electric heat
  - Comfortable sitting room
    - Complete privacy

LANSDOWNE
LODGE

Your hosts, Tom & Marion Kennedy,
Upper Stewiacke Valley,
Nova Scotia, B0N 2P0
(902) 268-2749

FRED A. WEBB AND SONS

Fred Webb and Sons are professional guides and outfitters operating in New Brunswick, Newfoundland and the Northwest Territories, offering a wide range of hunting, fishing and photographic expeditions.

In New Brunswick, clients are met by staff members in either Fredericton, New Brunswick or Presque Isle, Maine and are flown by bush plane or driven into the main lodge in Nictau. This 4,000-square mile hunting area has such a large black bear population hunters are allowed to shoot two per year – from early May until the end of June. They also have a large, healthy herd of big northern whitetails, some with wide racks sporting 10, 12 or more points and field dressing occasionally to 250 pounds or more. Deer season begins the first three weeks of October for bowhunters, followed by four weeks of regular rifle hunting. Either sex deer is allowed on a regular license.

In mid-September the hunt begins in Newfoundland where Fred is in partnership with one of the finest outfitters in the province. Here they offer a superb opportunity to hunt two major trophies – eastern Canada moose and woodland caribou. Newfoundland enjoys the densest moose population per square mile of any place in the world and hunting pressure is carefully controlled.

Hunters are flown into mountain plateau camps by bush plane from mid-September through October.

The company now has a partnership with MIKE FREELAND, operating out of Yellowknife, Northwest Territories. Over the years Qaivvik has hosted hundreds of hunters from all over the world, working with a number of Inuit communities to hunt central Canada barren ground caribou, muskox, polar bear and Peary caribou.

Fred Webb and Sons have provided years of high quality service to clients from all over the world. They have earned the reputation for first-class hunts and a high percentage of successful kills. Clients are guaranteed an enjoyable and exciting sporting experience.

FRED A. WEBB and SONS
RR1, PLASTER ROCK
NEW BRUNSWICK, CANADA E0J 1W0 (506) 356-8312

FRED A. WEBB & SONS

Fishing and Hunting New Brunswick Canada

FISH STORIES AND TALL TALES COME TRUE IN NEW BRUNSWICK

Forests and wilderness...lakes and streams...and some of the finest fishing rivers in the world make New Brunswick, Canada the place to be if you want your dreams to come true.

Fish for challenging smallmouth bass or the king of gamefish...the world renowned atlantic salmon.

Hunt for black bear, trophy whitetail and a variety of birds such as ruffed grouse and woodcock.

Relax and enjoy your stay in superb outfitting establishments where you become king of the New Brunswick outdoors.

Want to learn more...call toll free 1-800-561-0123.

ALCAMPO HUNTING ADVENTURES

Dr. Noriega y Garmendia 108
83000 Hermosillo, Sonora. MEXICO

Phone: (621) 2-32-39
Telex: FLFFME 58669

- **MULE DEER**

- **COUES DEER**

- **WHITE WING DOVE**

- **MOURNING DOVE**

- **QUAIL**

- **RED BILLED PIGEON**

HUNT MEXICO!

BOTSWANA

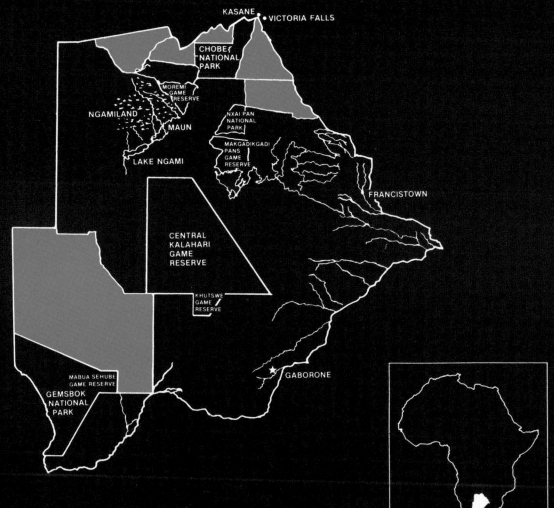

KASANE
• VICTORIA FALLS

CHOBE NATIONAL PARK

MOREMI GAME RESERVE

NGAMILAND

MAUN

NXAI PAN NATIONAL PARK

LAKE NGAMI

MAKGADIKGADI PANS GAME RESERVE

FRANCISTOWN

CENTRAL KALAHARI GAME RESERVE

KHUTSWE GAME RESERVE

MABUA SEHUBE GAME RESERVE

GEMSBOK NATIONAL PARK

★ GABORONE

Hunters Africa Concession Areas

Buffalo
Crocodile
Hartebeest
Kudu
Lechwe
Lion
Reedbuck
Tsessebe
Wildebeest
Bushbuck
Duiker
Gemsbok
Impala
Ostrich
Steinbock
Warthog
Eland
Springbok
Leopard
Sitatunga
Sable
Zebra

HUNTERS AFRICA
6 DESTA DRIVE
SUITE 5800
MIDLAND, TEXAS
79705 - 5510
A CLAYTON WILLIAMS JR. COMPANY

HUNTERS
AFRICA

VIA SARARIS is a family concern, and has been operating hunting safaris in Botswana since 1979. We offer YOU the excitement of Africa!

Ian, Ronnie and Allistair McFarlane are all professional hunters. They are well-known in Botswana and Africa for their experience, marksmanship and their excellent judgement of quality trophies.

SPECIES

Buffalo	Ostrich
Crocodile	Reedbuck
Eland	Sable
Gemsbok	Sitatunga
Hartebeeste	Springbok
Impala	Tsessebe
Kudo	Warthdog
Lechwe	Wildebeeste
Leopard	Zebra
Lion	

"Imagine a land of such variety that it boasts an incredible landlocked river delta the size of Switzerland, where herds of 3000 buffalo, 500 elephant and prides of 30 lion roam free in the manner born, and all this surrounded by the vast and harsh Kalahari Desert. But to merely imagine Botswana is not enough, for it is a treasurehouse of imaginable beauty, which can only be truly appreciated through personal experience."

VIRA SAFARIS (PTY) LTD

P.O. BOX 1602, GABORONE, BOTSWANA
TELEX NUMBER 2931 BD
TELEPHONE NUMBER (BUSINESS) 372308

VIRA
SAFARIS
LIMITED

"One of the last remnants of the Africa of which legends are made. Here time moves slowly, resisting the spoiling hand of man which has so changed the other lands once known by Rider Haggard, Livingstone and Courtenay Selous. Here the horizons are still endless, the night skies clear. The old mysteries still remain — pulsating on the floodwaters of the Okavango Delta, tranquil in the Kalahari Desert, where the bushmen still listen to the singing of the starts."

Botswana, politically stable and secure has the Okavango and the Kalahari to combine, to offer a unique diversity of wildlife.

PROFESSIONAL HUNTERS' ASSOCIATION OF SOUTH AFRICA

The Association's Aims and Objectives

To conserve game and flora

To safeguard the client and particularly the non-resident hunter

To promote the ethical conduct of hunting and to countenance only the fair chase

To maintain a high standard of professional service by members

Hunting with an association member assures your protection and enjoyment

Hunting in *South Africa*

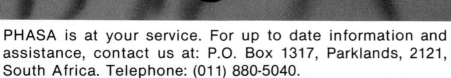

Hunting is what THABA'NKWE is all about. MAN — the hunter — testing his skills against that of the most cunning of animals. THABA'NKWE is your introduction to the true African Bushveld in all its harshness and beauty.

Here you step into a world where the lifestyle is in pace with the rythym of nature. Everything slows down — and one becomes aware of the sounds of the bush . . . Silence . . . bird calls . . . animal calls. One sees the surrounding fauna and flora with new eyes. Man now becomes aware of his own primitive needs. The hunting instinct comes alive and can follow its natural course — tracking — shooting and celebrating. Nothing can replace tradition and passion.

THABA'NKWE offers the greatest variety of indigenous species in any one country in the world.

The only country still offering THE BIG FIVE.

ACCOMMODATION

At THABA'NKWE each hunter will find a subtle blend of African hunting with gracious after-the-hunt living where warm and comfortable lodges are nestling in the Waterberg Mountains amid the picturesque streams and untouched nature. We are renowned for a personal and congenial atmosphere, exceptional cuisine, guaranteeing the hunter a memorable hunt.

The lodge is well equipped and adequately staffed to cater for the needs of the most discerning hunter and observer.

Our chef caters from either an open barbeque and lapa or a modern well equipped indoor kitchen.

Our lodges are designed to accommodate families, friends and hunting parties. A family tradition of personal service is guaranteed by the brothers KEN and MEL DU PLESSIS who are both qualified Professional Hunters, with an intimate knowledge of the fauna and flora of the African hunting grounds.

HUNTING SEASON AND DURATION

The hunting season is from April to October. Special hunts may be arranged outside these dates. Each hunt is planned to suit the personal requirements of the hunter, which normally runs from 7 to 21 days.

WEATHER AND CLOTHING

Days are usually mild to warm, however the early mornings and the evenings can be chilly. A daily laundry service is provided and hunters need not bring unnecessary clothing. We recommend the following — comfortable hunting boots — trousers or shorts if preferred — hunting hat or cap — clothing should be neutral or natural colours of the surroundings. For cooler weather a sweater or jacket will suffice.

HUNTING AREA

Most species can be taken on our Conservancy Areas in the famous savannahs of Northern Transvaal. This area was traditionally hunted by the big game hunters of Africa for many years.

Ken, Mel du Plessis of **Faunafrika**
P.O. Box 53, Vaalwater 0530, Rep. of South Africa
Tel: International (27) 11 683-4350 or (27) 15352 ask for 4202 or 4222
Telex: 489500 SA

Member of Safari Club International   **Registered Professional Hunters in terms of the laws of the Rep. of South Africa**   **Member of The Professional Hunters Association of South Africa**

FAUNAFRIKA

An organization dedicated to African Hunting and Hunting Safaris

Nothing can replace tradition and passion.

HUNTERS TRACKS
(Private) Limited

SAFARI

Glamorous old Africa of the explorers, early hunters and traders has largely disappeared; yet there are still certain regions known to the fortunate few, where the "story book" Africa still persists, where man has yet to make his mark and where roam countless thousands of wild animals.

For the visiting hunter certainly part of your safari is the fine sable, waterbuck, the nobly name lion, elephant, buffalo and the stealthy leopard silhouetted in your scope at sundown.

For the photographer, safari is the boundless opportunity to capture with your lens the most magnificent scenery and the greatest array of wildlife in the world.

Enjoyable, rewarding safaris become a reality when guided by men whose names are synonymous with all that is best in terms of skill and African bush lore.

Of course there's more, much more. But it is impossible to weave the enchanting spell of Africa into just a few words. However, we can promise you a fair crack at the trophies you seek, the numbers you want and the size and quality of which you have always dreamed.

So let us know your requirements, the numbers and types of game you want, when and for how long you'd like to stay and we'll give you a quote.

As for when you decide to come on safari we'll plan its every detail, reserve your game quotas. Look after you from the moment you arrive at the airport until the time you leave.

MEMBERS:
International Professional Hunters Association
Zimbabwe Professional Hunters Association
Game Conservation International
Safari Operators International
Safari Club International

P.O. Box CH 4, Chisipite, Zimbabwe
Cables: Trax, Telex: 4013 ZW
Phone: Arcturus 329 (Direct Line) Arcturus 27716 (Party Line)
Directors: A. R. Rowbotham, J. M. Rowbotham

REGISTERED BY THE GOVERNMENT OF ZIMBABWE AS CATEGORY ONE BIG GAME SAFARI OPERATORS

Fishing Fishing
Outfitters Outfitter
hing Fish
Fishing Fishing Fisl
hing Fishing Outfitte
Outfitters Outfitte
Outfitters Outfit
Fishing Fish
hing Fishing Outfi
Outfitters Outf
Fishing Fishing Out
Fishing Fishing Fisl
Outfitters Out
Fishing Outfitters Ou
Fishing Ou

Fishing Outfitters 2

DEEP SEA FISHING
FISH THE GREAT BARRIER REEF

Cairns, Australia is without doubt 'the marlin fishing capital of the world.' Fishermen come from all over the world each marlin season to fish for this great fighting fish. In addition the light tackle fishing is superb — sail fish, wahoo, mackerel, mai mai, tuna.

Bottom fishing in the shelter of the reef can be a gourmet delight — coral trout and red emperor are among the finest eating fish.

To experience the ultimate adventure, call or write:

World Hunts Inc., P.O. Box 777
Latrobe, Pennsylvania 15650
Tel: 412-537-7668   800-4-HUNTING
Telex: 4953951   FAX: 412-537-5301

Lynn Castle's UNALAKLEET RIVER LODGE

NORTHWEST ALASKA BERING SEA

King of the Salmon - June

Another great trip! Aug.

Four hundred air miles northwest of Anchorage, across the Yukon River to the shores of the fabled Bering Sea, lies a remote Eskimo village named Unalakleet (pronounced U-NA-LA-KLEET). Unlike most trophy fish areas in Alaska, there is no fishing competition from other lodges on the Unalakleet watershed. Nor must you fly out to enjoy really top Alaskan fishing, as we enjoy a wide variety of Alaska's finest sportfish right at our front door. The UNALAKLEET RIVER LODGE, is located a short 20-minute boat ride upriver from tidewater, making our fresh sea-run salmon some of the strongest and hardest fighting fish you will ever encounter. They are guaranteed to test your angling skill.

We kick off the season mid-June with one of the strongest King Salmon runs in the State, which normally extends through mid-July. These powerful and spirited ocean fresh monsters will average 25-30 pounds, with fish in the 50-60 pound class caught every season. That's a lot of fish in anyone's book!

As Winston Moore writes of the Unalakleet River in *The Pan Angler:* "It's the best I've been able to find for big fish."

In July, over one million Pink (Humpback) Salmon enter the Unalakleet River. Pinks aggressively take both lures and flies, earning them the reputation for striking "anything that hits the water." You can catch these fiesty fighters one after another "unti

your arms fall off." Can you think of a better way to spend a family vacation?

Beginning late June through mid-September, the hardiest and most colorful of the Pacific salmon family has made its way to our doorstep. The northern Chum (Calico) Salmon is unquestionably the most underrated of all of Alaska's game fish. While the average Calico weighs between 8-12 pounds, fish of 16 to 20 pounds are occasionally hooked. Pound for pound, this multicolored member of the salmon family will outfight any fish in Alaska, including the legendary Sheefish.

We enjoy one of the most intense Silver (Coho) Salmon runs in all Alaska. These famous hard-hitting, jumping fish enter the river late July and remain throughout September. Known for their aggressive striking characteristics, these 8-20 pound hunks of TNT readily take both lures and flies. Many experienced anglers feel that Silvers are the most exciting of all the Pacific salmon.

Very likely, the largest Arctic Grayling found in Alaska are Native to the clearwater streams and rivers entering the Bering Sea. And the Unalakleet drainages are literally loaded with these lovely "sailfish of the North." Averaging 2 to 2-½ pounds, guests have landed several monsters weighing in excess of 4 pounds, and 24 inches in length! It is just a matter of time before a UNALAKLEET RIVER LODGE guest catches the new Alaskan World Record Grayling. . . . And it could be you!

Throughout the summer months, schools of brilliantly colored Arctic Char, and their silvery cousins, the Dolly Varden, move in and out of the river following the various runs of salmon. Average size of these excellent eating beauties runs 3-6 pounds. During the last week of July and the first week of August, Char and Dollies swarm by the tens of thousands into jthe Unalakleet's salmon spawning beds. At this time fishing is literally "a fish a cast" on both flies and lures.

Fishing on the Unalakleet is conducted from river boats equipped with either prop and/or jet driven Mercury outboards. Normally each boat is limited to two guests and their personal guide. Catch and release, while not a hardfast rule, is practiced on most species, particularly in the upper tributaries when fishing for trophy grayling.

The Unalakleet River boasts the heaviest salmon runs in the Bering Sea fishery, and is spawning home to literally millions of fish: mighty Kings, fiesty Pink Salmon, the explosive Calico or Chum Salmon, and fighting Silvers, in addition to trophy-sized Arctic Grayling, Dolly Varden and Arctic Char. In addition, our optional fly-out program offers trophy Northern Pike and Sheefish.

Originally the showcase lodge of the Silvertip group, UNALAKLEET RIVER LODGE now operates under the very capable leadership of Master Guide and pilot Lynn and Penny Castle, who for more than twenty-four years, have built a reputation unequaled in Alaskan wilderness circles. Their goal is to offer guests unequalled hospitality and fishing adventure in Northwestern Alaskan waters.

UNALAKLEET RIVER LODGE offers its guests maximum care and service. The total staff-to-guest ratio is among the highest of any Alaskan lodge, and includes one full-time fishing guide per each two clients. Our guides are hand-picked professionals, most of whom have worked with Lynn for many years. We do not believe in booking the largest number of persons possible. Our schedule is arranged so that personal attention may be given to every guest, to insure not only successful fishing, but a memorable and enjoyable trip as well.

At UNALAKLEET RIVER LODGE we take great Alaskan style meals one step further. Awaken in your room to a pot of steaming coffee or piping hot tea, followed by a breakfast fit for a King. Aftrer an exciting morning on the river you'll typically enjoy a "shore lunch" prepared by your personal guide from your morning's catch. Mouth watering Dolly Varden, or perhaps a 'just caught' salmon, baked potatoes, roasted corn, fruit, garlic bread, and white wine or beer all take on a special flavor in your scenic wilderness surroundings.

At day's end settle in front of the warm fireplace or handcarved bar for hor d'ouevres and 'happy hour', to share your day's adventures with friends . . . both old and new. Then venture to the summit of Alaska lodge dinners, including char-broiled New York steaks, traditional English prime ribs, or perhaps a full Thanksgiving-style turkey with all the trimming's.

We invite you to join us, to experience Northwest Alaska's finest wilderness fishing. UNALAKLEET RIVER LODGE is beyond expectations — and it's all there waiting for you!

Arctic Char • July - Sept.

Silver Salmon • Aug. - Sept.

Included as part of the regular lodge program is the opportunity to visit a comfortable wilderness tent camp accessibly only by jet-boat and/or aircraft. Typically these camps include your guide(s), private sleeping tents with cots and mattresses, dining tent, cook and radio communications.

Rates INCLUDE lodging based on shared accommodations, guide services, meals, one overnight excursion to wilderness tent camp, and transportation

between Unalakleet and the lodge. Unalakleet is serviced daily by major airlines from Anchorage and Nome. Group rates apply throughout season on space available basis. Special family discounts available during late July.

Whether with family or friends, or your next business meeting, we invite you to come with us and experience Northwestern Alaskan fishing at its best!

Fishing and Hunting New Brunswick Canada

FISH STORIES AND TALL TALES
COME TRUE IN NEW BRUNSWICK

Forests and wilderness...lakes and streams...and some of the finest fishing rivers in the world make New Brunswick, Canada the place to be if you want your dreams to come true.

Fish for challenging smallmouth bass or the king of gamefish...the world renowned atlantic salmon.

Hunt for black bear, trophy whitetail and a variety of birds such as ruffed grouse and woodcock.

Relax and enjoy your stay in superb outfitting establishments where you become king of the New Brunswick outdoors.

Want to learn more...call toll free 1-800-561-0123.

NOVAS

Sleek silver Nova Scotia salmon glide in from the sea to join four species of resident spotted trout in the lakes and streams. Then, shimmering American shad join the migration and, behind them, come the seatrout back from rich feeding in the estuaries. By summer, smallmouth bass will be active in the warm water lakes and, by fall, giant stripers will have entered fresh water . . .

Be ready for them. Book early with one of the outfitters listed below.

A modern, secluded lodge on an eight acre island providing a full line of services for trout and salmon fishing, and bird, bear and deer hunting.

Call or write for details: Don Breen
P.O. Box 402, Milton, Queens County, Nova Scotia,
B0T 1P0
(902) 354-4354

Accommodation for 4-6 overlooking the magnificent Lake Bras d'Or. One licensed guide for every two people. Hunting for rabbit, waterfowl, upland birds and our specialty — white tail deer. Great fishing for salmon, rainbow, speckled and brown trout.

Contact: Earl Rudderham
RR #2 Boisdale, Christmas Island
Cape Breton, Nova Scotia, B0A 1C0
(902) 871-2549

Comfortable accommodations and experienced guide service for brook and lake trout, bass fishing. Hunting guides for showshoe hare, upland and big game including white tail deer and black bear.

Contact: Robert & Marie Gauthier
RR#2, Annapolis County, Nova Scotia, B0S 1A0
(902) 638-3509

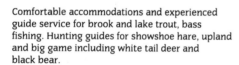

Quality guiding, comfortable lodgings and hearty meals in the middle of some of the finest trout and salmon fishing, and big game hunting anywhere.

Contact: Aubrey R. Beaver
P.O. Box 40, Sherbrooke, Nova Scotia, B0J 3C0
(902) 522-2235

Knowledgeable outfitting services for Atlantic salmon, brown trout, upland birds and big game in one of Nova Scotia's most outstanding lodges.

Contact: Tom & Marion Kennedy
Upper Stewiacke Valley, Nova Scotia, B0N 2P0
(902) 671-2749

A fully equipped, modern lodge with salmon and salt water fishing close by. Guide service and equipment rentals available.

Contact: The Manager
N.S. Department of Tourism, P.O. Box 456, Halifax,
Nova Scotia, B3J 2R5
(902) 779-2307 (summer) (902) 424-5000 (winter)

COTIA

We offer some of the best salmon fishing and accommodations in North America on the famous, spectacular Margaree River, acknowledged as perhaps the most beautiful salmon stream on the continent.

Please contact: David MacDonald, Owner,
P.O. Box 178, Margaree Valley, Nova Scotia, B0E 2C0
(902) 248-2987

Single party bookings in each of our two lodges and one guide for every two hunters ensure privacy for hunting upland birds, white tail deer and black bear.

Write or call: Roger & Anna Ehrenfeld
P.O. Box 149, Middleton, Nova Scotia, B0S 1P0
(902) 825-4030 (days) or (902) 825-6629 (evenings)

Salmon and trout fishing in two famous streams, hunting for upland birds, waterfowl and big game from a comfortable, secluded lodge on the Medway River.

Call or write: Moyal Conrad
Greenfield, Queens County, Nova Scotia, B0T 1E0
(902) 685-2423 (lodge) (902) 685-2378/2376

SENTINEL SAFETY CONSULTANTS

Outfitting services for fishing and hunting — smallmouth & striped bass, salmon, ducks, geese and white tail deer in the Annapolis Valley and the South Shore of Nova Scotia.

Please call or write: Ron Seney
Meisner's Section, RR#3, New Germany, Nova Scotia,
B0R 1E0 (902) 644-3015

Experienced guides, home cooked meals and private hunting land for snowshoe hare, white tail deer, black bear and fishing for Atlantic salmon and brown trout.

Please contact: David & Linda Kennedy
RR#3, Brookfield, Colchester County, Nova Scotia, B0N 1C0
(902) 673-2023

Two secluded cabins on the St. Mary's River providing guides for trout and salmon fishing and white tail deer hunting.

Contact: Phillip Turner
RR#1, Aspen, Guysborough County, Nova Scotia, B0H 1E0
(902) 833-2303

Jack MacIsaac
Minister of Tourism

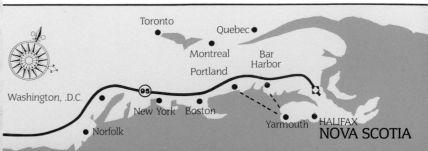

the thrill of fishing in
wilderness lakes . . .
for northern pike,
arctic grayling,
rainbow and lake trout.

DICK & HOLLY SMITH • OUTFITTERS
INDIAN RIVER RANCH
GUIDES and OUTFITTERS
P.O. BOX 165, ATLIN, B.C., CANADA
V0W 1A0 SUMMER 604•651•7515
WINTER 503•987•2123

Booking Agents Agents Agents Booking Booking Booking Agents Agents Booking Booking Agents Agents Booking Booking Agents Agents Booking Booking Agents

Booking Agents 3

NORTH AMERICAN GRAND SLAM HUNTS

4 Bear

4 Caribou

4 Deer

4 Sheep

arrange your next hunt with Rick Furniss ''a hunt consultant who has been there''

WORLD HUNT SERVICES LTD.
RICK FURNISS

Hunt Consultant & Professional Hunter
Box 5364, Whitehorse, Yukon, Canada Y1A 4Z2
403-667-2712

SPECIALITY HUNTS AND CONSULTING SERVICES

I provide a consulting service for anyone interested in arranging a hunt for any species of game in North America. This service is only provided on a very personal basis over the phone. Like my Yukon Outfitting business, I offer this service to a small number of very special clients.

I personally escort a few select clients on very special hunts all over North America, Africa, Mexico & Europe.

I am one of only 11 people who has successfully hunted **all** 27 North American Big Game Animals. I am recognized as a world authority for North America Big Game Hunting. I have been the special North American Technical Consultant to the Record Committee for Safari Club International.

If you wish to arrange a hunt through me you must send a deposit to me. Upon receipt of a deposit I finalize a reservation for you with an outfitter I know is reputable. I will thoroughly discuss the details with you prior to committing your deposit to any outfitter. If you are considering a hunt soon, anywhere, for any species, then let my knowledge and experience work for you to get the best hunt available.

Rick Furniss
Professional Hunt Consultant

WORLDWIDE HUNTING, FISHING PHOTOGRAPHIC & ADVENTURE SAFARIS

SATOUR

World Hunts Inc., a full service booking agency, is now offering trips to these areas:

NORTH AMERICA	SOUTH PACIFIC
AFRICA	Australia
Botswana	New Zealand
Namibia	New Guinea
South Africa	ASIA
Tanzania	
Zambia	EUROPE
Zimbabwe	SOUTH AMERICA

To experience the ultimate adventure, call or write:
World Hunts Inc.
P.O. Box 777
Latrobe, Pennsylvania 15650
Tel: 412-537-7668
    800-4-HUNTING
Telex: 4953951
FAX: 412-537-5301

Rifles & Rifles Accessories & Rifles & Rifles Accessories & Rifles & Rifles Accessories & Rifles & Rifles Accessories & Rifles & Rifles Accessories

Rifles & Rifles Accessories 4

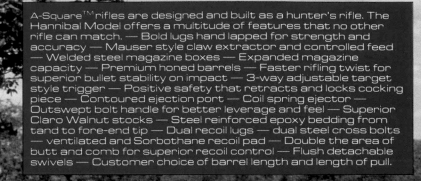

Blaser

Single Shot Rifle
Modell K 77 A

The Blaser K 77 A
Superb accuracy, mountain climbing weight, magnum power, suitcase portability and safety are some of the features of the Blaser break action single shot rifle.
Advanced new technology allows a break action single shot to have the strength and accuracy of a bolt action rifle.
This fine single shot easily uses the worlds most powerful cartridges and is capable of handling the highest industries standard chamber pressures. Lifespan of the rifle with 7 mm Mag. or 300 Weath. cartridges is almost unlimited. All of this in one of the lightest weight rifles ever produced in the world – 5½ lbs.

See your local Blaser Dealer
or write to us for complete details.

Autumn Sales Inc.
1320 Lake Street
Fort Worth, TX 76102
Ph. (817) 335-1634

Blaser

Blaser Jagdwaffen GmbH
7972 Isny/Allgäu
West Germany
Ph. 07562-7020

96

BY APPOINTMENT TO H.R.H. THE DUKE OF EDINBURGH
RIFLE MAKERS HOLLAND & HOLLAND LTD LONDON

HOLLAND & HOLLAND ARE NOW KNOWN FOR MORE THAN THEIR GUNS AND RIFLES

For over one hundred and fifty years Holland
& Holland big game and stalking rifles have been
used all over the world — from the Highlands of
Scotland and the Himalayas to the jungles of India,
Africa and South America and in the frozen wastes of
the North American continent. Today, in addition to
their world renowned guns and rifles, Holland & Holland
offer a complete range of shooting clothing and accessories.
The instructors from the Holland & Holland Shooting School,
who make frequent instructional visits to America, have a deserv-
edly high reputation. A visit to Holland & Holland will help you to
prepare for every kind of hunting expedition. Please write for our new
Gun and Rifle Price Lists, our Shooting and Clothing and Accessories
Catalogue and the Holland & Holland Shooting School folder.

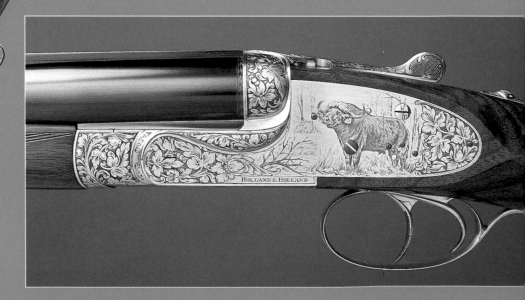

HOLLAND & HOLLAND

LIMITED

33 Bruton Street, London W1X 8JS

Telephone 01-499 4411   *Telex* 269021 GUNNER G

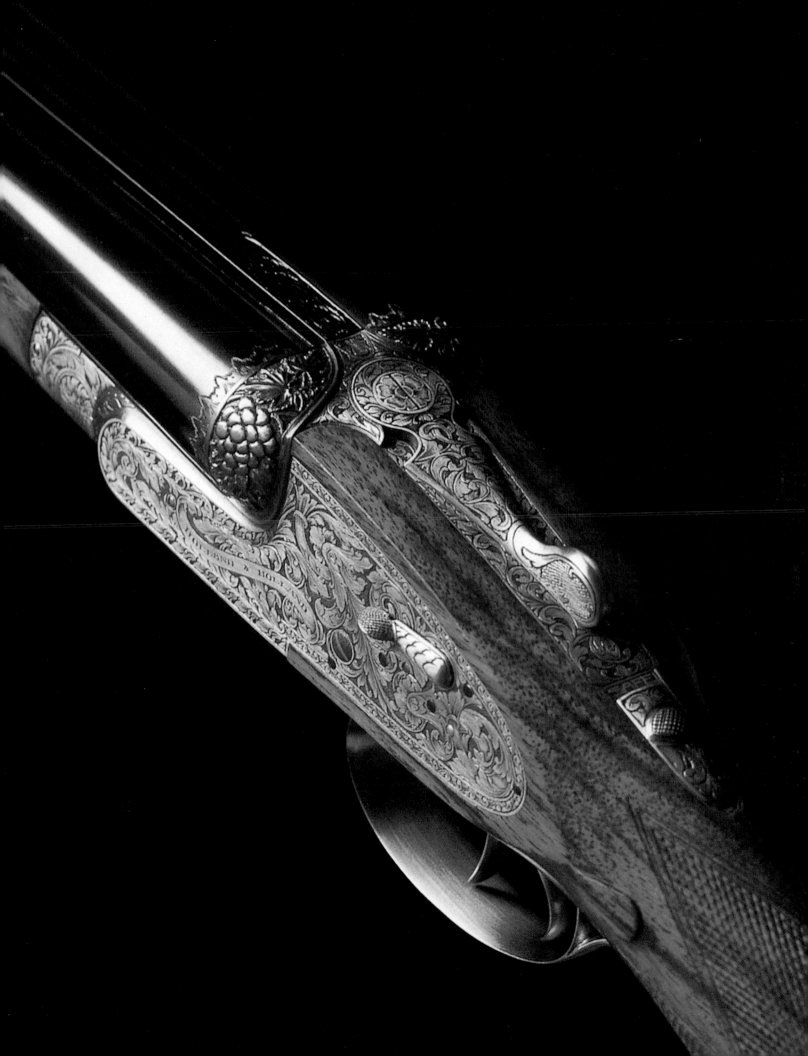

NOISE EXPOSURE

How it Affects Your Hearing

By Deborah R. Price, M.S., CCC/A

Noise exposure to the ear is defined as a product of the acoustic intensity of sound and the duration of sound; a measure summarizing the amount of acoustic energy that has entered the ear canal and is received by the inner ear. The harmful affects of the noise exposure are cumulative. A hearing loss might not occur overnight, but generally would build up over a period of years. The physiological response to noise is an individualized reaction. Danger or damage threshold for an individual may be 65 dBA while another may not sustain injury or disfunction until 100 dBA. OSHA has set a limit of 85 dBA as a starting point for ear protection. For the hunter noise exposure differs from that of the work place. Hunters are not typically exposed to continuous high noise levels. The hunter is exposed to impulse noise.

Impulse noise can be described as one or more short, transient, acoustical events which last less than .5 seconds. It has been observed that repeated exposure to acoustic impulse noise exceeding peak levels of 140 dB could result in significant loss of hearing. 120 dB is generally accepted as the maximum intensity level tolerated for safety. Sounds reaching 130 dB may cause discomfort, 135 dB causes a tickling sensation in the ear and 140 dB usually results in pain. There is usually a trade off between the intensity of the pulse and the number of pulses that can be experienced. A change of 10 dB in the peak level will result in a different number of impulses acceptable as safe

by a factor of 10. Assuming a base of 100 impulses, if the peak level was 150 dB, then only 10 pulses per day might be considered safe. This is critical to the hunter as the number of firings and loudness level is not always predictable.

There are two main types of hearing loss resulting from noise exposure. One is hearing loss that occurs gradually over a period of years. The other type of hearing loss is attributable to a single, brief but intense exposure to noise. A common way to describe the affects of noise exposure involves a discussion of auditory threshold of hearing. Threshold of hearing is defined as the minimum affective sound pressure of a signal that is capable of evoking an auditory sensation. Stated differently, the softest sound recognized and detected by the human ear. Audiometrically, (for diagnostic and testing purposes) threshold is recorded as the intensity of a tone at which an individual will, upon hearing the stimulus, respond 50% of the time. Audiometric thresholds are reported in dB with a 0 dB being the average hearing level of normal adults with no otologic pathology (ear problems) or history of noise trauma. The classic audiometric manifestation of hearing loss as a result of noise exposure is a 40 dB loss at 4,000 Hz. With greater exposure to loud noise, the gap between normal hearing and a moderate loss grows deeper and broader with high frequencies affected more rapidly than low frequencies until finally high frequency perception of sound is lost. This results in an inability

to hear consonant sounds like s, f, p, t, v, th, sh.

Temporary Threshold Shift (TTS) is a phrase used to describe a short term affect resulting in decreased hearing which follows an exposure to noise; but the hearing sensitivity recovers gradually following the noise exposure. Permanent Threshold Shift (PTS) defines decreased hearing changes which persist throughout the lifetime of the affected person. Baseline auditory threshold information should be established prior to noise exposure. A measurement then taken following the exposure will demonstrate the shift that has occurred as a result of the noise exposure. At this point, the shift may be temporary. Recovery to baseline may not always be full recovery but should occur. If there is no recovery to baseline the loss is permanent. Stated another way, the loss in hearing sensitivity as a result of chronic noise exposure is called "Noise Induced Temporary Threshold Shift" if the decrease in sensitivity eventually disappears. However, loss is called a "Noise Induced Permanent Threshold Shift" if there is no recovery. Noise with energy concentrated in the 2,000 - 6,000 Hz. range produce more temporary threshold shifts than noise with energy elsewhere in the frequency spectrum. Therefore, high frequency noise exposure is more injurious to the ear than low frequency noise exposure.

An ear that has already sustained sensorineural hearing loss (permanent loss of hearing) will show less threshold shift as a result of noise exposure than a normal ear. The ear with sensori-neural loss will require more signal energy for hearing than the normal ear following a shift. The acquisition of a permanent loss of hearing from noise cannot be considered protection against any further loss. The noise damaged ear is more susceptible to further injury than an undamaged ear. Although less threshold shift occurs, a sound must be even louder for the affected ear to hear as a result of the shift. It is unknown whether the very young or the very aged person is more susceptible to noise damage and these threshold shifts.

When an individual has experienced a TTS or PTS as a result of noise exposure it is manifest as a difficulty in understanding conversation in the presence of background noise. There may also be a muffling of speech and changes in the quality of other sounds. Head noises or ringing, referred to as tinnitus, frequently accompany noise exposure. Tinnitus may be a high pitched ringing, cricket sounds, ocean roar, or any number of head noises.

An effective way to protect the ear from noise induced damage is through the use of ear protectors. Two types of ear protection are available. One type of protection is the ear muff which is worn over the external ear providing an acoustic seal against the head. The other type is insert ear plugs which seal off the entrance to the ear canal. Ear muffs although bulky and heavy provide the maximum amount of protection to the ear. They should always be used when target shooting or on the rifle range. Insert type ear plugs are better used in the field. It is important to note that no single size plug can be found that will fit the large range of ear canal sizes and shapes. Custom molded ear plugs are preferable. Custom ear plugs are available that will totally occlude sound from entering the ear. Unfortunately many hunters will remove one of the ear plugs in order to carry on a conversation. When this occurs, the ear exposed may sustain a TTS or PTS as a result of the noise from other hunters. A type of custom ear plug is now available that has a sound channel bored through the ear mold. Inserted in the sound channel is an acoustic filter which engages in the presence of loud noise. This type of custom ear plug will enable the hynter to carry on a conversation without removing the ear plug and still protect him/her against the damage from noise exposure. It is important to note that ear protectors should fit properly. Poor fitting noise protection devices are worse than none at all as they give the wearer a false sense of security without solving the problem. Wearing only one earphone or loose fitting ear plug is not helpful. The chief problem has been in motivating hunters to wear ear protection.

Should an individual notice a change in hearing as a result of noise exposure, contact an audiologist, a specialist in testing and rehabilation of hearing impaired individuals, or an otologist, a doctor specializing in diseases of the ear. If a hearing loss already exists it does not mean the individual is safe from further injury. Always wear some type of ear protection when in the presence of loud noise. Hearing is a precious gift to be valued and protected.

Deborah Price is the owner and founder of Hearing Professional Center. She is a licensed audiologist and has been serving the needs of central Dallas for more than seven years. Receiving her Bachelor of Science Magna Cum Laud from the University of Texas at Dallas, she completed a Master of Science in Communication Disorders in 1980. Ms. Price is licensed by the State of Texas and completed her Certificate of Clinical Competence in 1981. Ms. Price serves as an Adjunct Faculty at the University of Texas at Dallas and is the founder of a philanthropic organization, Deaf Services International serving the needs of deaf children in Mexico.

Ms. Price is an active member of several professional organizations, both state and national, and is a frequent presenter at annual conventions. She also holds a yearly exhibit at the Dallas Safari Club Convention providing information to hunters at large.

Hearing Professional Center, 5477 Glen Lakes Drive, Suite 106, Dallas, Texas 75231, (214) 987-4114.

Scopes & Binoculars Binoculars Scopes & Scopes & Scopes Binoculars Binoculars Scopes & Scopes & Scopes Binoculars Binoculars Scopes & Scopes

Scopes & Binoculars 5

SWAROVSKI
OPTIK

SLC COMPACT BINOCULARS

When you're on the move, you need precision binoculars with real portability. The new Swarovski SLC Compacts. Lightweight and small sized, they provide the high resolution only the finest European optics can offer.

Because they're built with a sturdy outer casing, they don't need a bulky carrying case. That means you can stash these binoculars almost anywhere—glove compartment, knapsack, even a purse.

Waterproof.
Shockproof.
Fogproof.
Dustproof.
Fungusproof.

Dependable for life.

TANZANIA. BOTSWANA. SWAROVSKI.

Names you'll never forget.

You know the names that mean great African hunting. They may have sounded peculiar at first, but now they're a part of your language.

The same goes for Swarovski (Swar-ov-skee). Once you've used these riflescopes and binoculars, you'll never forget the name—because they deliver the same high performance and reliability that you expect from all your equipment.

We start with fine European optics. Laser-aligned, they provide high resolution and clarity, even in the lowest light. And they're protected by casings built for protection.

Swarovski riflescopes are strong enough to take the rough treatment of a trophy hunt on any continent. Regardless of recoil or caliber size, they always deliver dependable accuracy.

Swarovski SLC Compact binoculars are just as rugged. They start out the best and stay that way for a lifetime. From first light until night they deliver the highest resolution and clarity, regardless of the temperature or humidity.

Riflescopes and binoculars that mean great hunting. Swarovski. Use them once and you'll never forget the name.

For your free booklet "How to Select Binoculars" and the name of your nearest Swarovski dealer, write:

Swarovski Optik
Dept.: CS
One Kenney Drive
Cranston, Rhode Island 02920

Swarovski Canada Limited
3781 Victoria Park Avenue
Unit 8
Scarborough, Ontario
M1W 3K5

SWAROVSKI OPTIK

Ammunition & Accessories Ammunition & Accessories Ammunition & Accessories Ammunition & Accessories Ammunition & Accessories Ammunition & Accessories Ammunition & Accessories

Ammunition 6 & Accessories

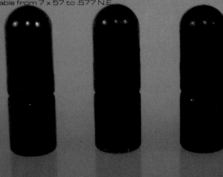
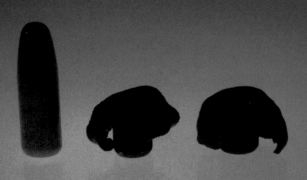

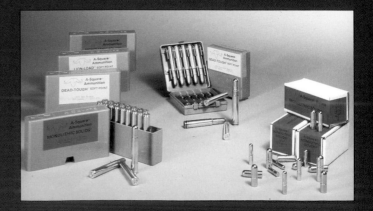

The growing popularity of Federal shotshells is causing some pheasants to trade in their wings for running shoes. And who can blame them — Federal shotshells are powerful stuff.

Federal makes a huge assortment of hard-hitting shotshell ammunition for whatever game you're after. So whether you choose our moderately priced Duck & Pheasant loads or our copper-plated Premium™ brand Hi-Power® loads, you can be assured of one thing — full, dense, deadly patterns.

But don't be surprised if the pheasants respond by keeping a very low profile. You'd probably do the same if you were in their shoes.

FEDERAL®
GO HUNTING WITH FEDERAL,
THE DRIVING FORCE IN AMMUNITION

"If they're gonna switch to Federal Shotshells, I'm gonna switch to running!"

Federal Cartridge Company, Anoka, MN 55303.

MADE IN THE U.S.A.

© 1987 FCC

Take aim. You've got the best ammunition money can buy.

The fact is, some brands of ammunition work better than others. And none works better than Federal.

Federal Hi-Shok® centerfires combine all the ingredients you need for success. Hard-hitting Hi-Shok bullets feature a special design that delivers mushroom expansion up to 200% of the original bullet diameter. The resulting knockdown power is incredible.

When you finally get that once-in-a-lifetime shot, make certain your ammunition is up to the task. Make certain it's Federal.

FEDERAL ®
THE DRIVING FORCE IN AMMUNITION
Federal Cartridge Company, Minneapolis, MN 55402

MADE IN THE U.S.A.

Notes Notes

Supplies Supplies

Supplies 7

When I need my photo taken . . .
I give my guide my CONTAX camera

Sherman Hines

Contax photo by Sherman Hines from his photographic exposé, 'The North'

When you want quality results — think Contax/Zeiss T*. Sherman does.

FROM THE ROCKIES...

SHERMAN HINES INSISTS
ON USING FUJICHROME FOR SUPERB COLOR AND CLARITY

TO THE MOUNTAINS OF CHINA...

ACTION-PACKED
VIDEO CASSETTES
Brilliantly photographed and
narrated by Sportsman/Photographer
George Klucky

As the man behind the camera, George Klucky narrates each adventure as it unfolds . . . the triumphs, the disappointments, the touches of humor. These videos are unique . . . the **real thing** . . . no faked sequences. George Klucky captures the "moment of truth" between the hunter and his quarry.

VIDEO TAPES NOW AVAILABLE
African Safari with Irvin Barnhart
Where the Salmon and Trout are King
Spring Black Bear in NB Canada with Al King
The Challenge of the Eastern Wild Turkey
Ruger Presents Alaska
Utah Mountain Lion
Trophy Caribou Hunting
Johny Johnson's Big 4 Safari
Lord of the Tundra
Thomas & Thomas Presents Labrador
Alaskan Rainbow Trout and Silver Salmon
Riley's Alaskan Brown Bear
Lynn Castles, Unalakeet River Lodge, Alaska
Hunting with Larry Rivers, Alaska
Grizzly and Moose Hunting in the Talkeetna Mtns., Alaska

ORDER FROM: Wilderness Adventures
22 Crosier Ave, Pittsfield, Mass. 01201
(413) 443-1510

1-800-338-1970

GEORGE KLUCKY
Throughout his life George pursued his interest in nature and the sport of hunting and fishing. His travels through North America, Canada and Africa expanded his awareness of others who shared his enthusiasm. In 1969 George started filming his adventures and those of his colleagues. Klucky's footage has appeared on television in the United States and Canada. His films are backed by narration with music highlighting the sound track of the events and catches he captures on film. George is a renowned guest speaker, presenting his films and experiences to sports clubs and fund raisers. He's a regular on national television wildlife programs and is a reoccuring guest on *Call of the Outdoors, Cabin Fever,* and *Woods and Waters.* His films are currently on tour throughout Canada and the Northeastern United States.

GEORGE KLUCKY

WILDERNESS ADVENTURES

ACTION PACKED HUNTING AND FISHING FILMS . . .

"Klucky never misses the shot."
Ted Williams
Renown Fly Fisherman

UNALAKLEET RIVER LODGE

Dear Sportsman,

The North American Outdoorsman is proud to present, to you, the most exciting and highest production-quality videos in the marketplace today. N.A.O.'s cameras will go afield, each year, to bring home the beauty and excitement we all seek and share in the great outdoors. Our programs are committed to portraying sound conservation practices and good sportsmanship, as well.

At last, affordable, high adventure, high quality outdoor videos within reach of all who love the land and water, and all it has to offer. Comments from our viewers will continue to serve as a guideline for the subject matter of our future shows. The North American Outdoorsman's pledge is to provide the type and quality videos you deserve.

Arnold Alward
President

Rocky Mountain Rainbows and Arctic Goose Hunt

High in Alberta's Canadian Rockies for Rainbow Trout provides action so fast above and below the surface you will be reaching for a net.

We then head north to James Bay to hunt Blue Geese. The Cree Indian guides will share with you proven hunting methods that have stood the test of time.

Three Trout to Dream About and Minipi's Discovery

On a single cast with three flies on his leader, Lee Wulff hooks and then lands three great Brook Trout totalling seventeen pounds in weight.

In Minipi's Discovery, you will fly into that great fishing area with Lee in his seaplane when he alone had cast a fly in those magnificent trout waters.

Flashing Silver

The Queen Charlotte Islands off British Columbia lie in the path of the annual Coho migration. These great bays and inlets provide fly fishermen with the type of action that separate fish tales from fantasies. You'll witness a majestic Bald Eagle that competes with the anglers for these silvery beauties. Unbelievable jumping action and spectacular underwater photography.

San Juan River Tarpon and A World Record Marlin

Fly fish for Tarpon with Jack Nicklaus, Curt Gowdy and Lee Wulff and watch two young native lads take one in their own inimitable style.

Lee Wulff takes a world's record Striped Marlin, on a fly, in Ecuador and lands a 148 pounder on a twelve pound test leader tippet. Narrated by Curt Gowdy.

Dead River Rough Cut

Two Maine woodsmen in a remote wilderness area...living in the last tarpaper remains of a former German prisoner of war camp, hunting, trapping, and logging with a team of oxen. Running counterpoint to the sync-action of the movie are their reflections on women, politics, death and taxes. Red Ribbon, American Film Festival. (some profanity).

Leaping Silver and Atlantic Salmon Angling Techniques

Joan Wulff demonstrates the fine art of fly casting for Atlantic Salmon on a Labrador river. Lee Wulff shows his techniques for playing, landing and releasing a 24 lb. salmon taken on a #16 fly.

Autumn Silver

In Autumn Silver, Joan and Lee Wulff fish for Atlantic Salmon on a Nova Scotia river, the Stewiake, in October when the fall foliage is at its peak, as brilliant as the leaps of the salmon. You'll see good casting, high leaping fish, and a beautiful sequence of fishing in a silvery fog that drifts in from the sea. This film won the "Teddy" award as Best Fishing Film of 1980.

Moose and Caribou in Newfoundland

Lee Wulff hunts the wild interior of the island of Newfoundland for the native Caribou and the lordly Moose. Go out to hunt each day from a lonely tent camp and thrill to the sight of the great game animals in their unspoiled terrain. A beautiful hunting film with great shots of magnificent animals.

With Camera and Gun in Newfoundland

Camera and Gun in Newfoundland lets the viewer judge whether Lee Wulff, the hunter, or his wife, the photographer, has the best of the sport. They end up with both steaks and photographs...among them one of the only known pictures of white Bull Moose. Magnificent shots of Moose and Caribou to be enjoyed by hunter and non-hunter alike.

The Way it Was: Angling in Newfoundland, 1938-1940

You'll see wild trout in schools, sea-run Brook Trout and the magnificent spectacle of the once fabulous run of salmon leaping Humber Falls. This is a film to make old-timers remember what it was like "back then" and newer generations wish they could, somehow, have been there to enjoy it.

Big Northern Pike

Northern Ontario when seen from the air seems to have more water than land. Lee and Joan Wulff fly into this great wilderness with big Walleye and Northern Pike on their mind. Sinclair Cheechew will host our visiting anglers on Kesagami Lake where the water is always cool and fishing hot!

Where the Biggest Bluefins Swim

The present World's record tuna was caught in the Strait of Canso in the Province of Nova Scotia. Lee Wulff, then in his 77th year, will show you that catching big tuna is not just a young man's game, but one of skill and endurance rather than great strength. Lee lands a 960 pounder on a 130-lb. test line. This film won the "Teddy" as best fishing film for 1983.

THE NORTH AMERICAN OUTDOORSMAN ®

THE NORTH AMERICAN OUTDOORSMAN® Video Selections

Whitetail
In Whitetail we join Lee Wulff on a deer hunt in the fall splendor of the New England woods. Share in the lore of hunting with Lee and then the drama and excitement as he stalks a rare and elusive White Buck, while his companion experiences the frustrations and final triumph of his first hunt. Some of the finest Whitetail footage ever filmed.

Soliloquy to a Salmon and The Atlantic Salmon
Soliloquy to a Salmon reflects Lee Wulff's thoughts as he plays and releases an eighteen pound Atlantic Salmon on Quebec's St. Jean River. Many consider this 1965 "Teddy" award winning film to be Lee's finest. Lee also brings in a seventeen pound fish using only the three foot tip of his fly rod to accomplish it. This takes place in beautiful Newfoundland.

Courageous Lake Caribou
The barren grounds in Canada's N.W.T. liven when the Bathurst herd migrates south. Leonard Clarke harvests a fine trophy and Albert Fish dresses it in a manner seldom seen in the outside world. You'll see virgin fishing for Lake Trout, Pike and Arctic Grayling. The action above and below the surface will have you wiping the smell of fish from your hands.

Giant Tuna, Small Boat
Travel with Lee Wulff to the coastal waters of Newfoundland's Notre Dame Bay. You'll see Lee troll for these great sea rovers from a sixteen foot Boston Whaler and hook and land a 650 pound Bluefin on an 80 lb. test line. Follow their small boat far offshore into a storm as they finally capture and release another great Bluefin out where the icebergs drift down from Labrador.

Big 3 in Newfoundland
It's the peak of the rut and the moose are on the move! Woodland Caribou are getting herding tendencies, and Black Bear are at their peak weight. Arnold Alward is in pursuit of a trophy Bull Moose. Bob Costas is licensed for all three big game animals. Their hardy trek over the Long Range Mountains will etch exciting memories, not only for themselves, but for all those who view this exciting video.

Ungava Char
Ungava Bay is an inland sea in northern Quebec's sub-Arctic. The Payne and Tunilik Rivers feed this great bay and provide a watery highway for Arctic Char returning to spawn. Russ Carpenter and Sammy Cantafio take you above and below the surface to witness the evasive action that Char are famous for.

To Ecuador for Marlin
Joan and Lee Wulff probe the Humbolt Current for Striped Marlin and Pacific Sailfish. Joan plays a Striped Marlin that makes fifteen consecutive jumps in a single run of the camera. Share the excitement when Lee casts to surfacing marlin with a light outfit, his thrill when he hooks a big Black Marlin on his light tackle.

Upland Gunner
Go afield in the grouse and woodcock coverts of Maine's colorful autumn, to a Georgia plantation to see coveys of quail roar into flight over a fine pointing dog, hunt ringneck pheasants in Oregon where that great game bird was introduced to America. See excellent dog work and shotgunning at a snow-covered game farm in Missouri.

Atlantic Salmon at Helen's Falls
The George River in Quebec's sub-Arctic draws one of the largest migrations of salmon in North America plus a migration of outdoor notables like Gene Hill, Jim Rikhoff and Tom Hennessey who cast their flies in pursuit of this silvery treasure. Arctic Char will thrill the viewer with the fastest surface and underwater action ever filmed.

The Fly Fisherman's World
Travel with Lee Wulff to Montana to fish for trout with a delicate six foot fly rod, and to Labrador where he challenges a great Atlantic Salmon on the same featherweight rod. Join him in the Florida Keys to land a hundred and thirty pound Tarpon and continue on to Pinas Bay, Panama, to share the thrill of playing and subduing a high leaping, deep diving, Pacific Sailfish.

Mistassini for Me
Art and Kris Lee share the happiness and heartbreaks when fishing for trophy Northern Pike. Charley Jolly takes you below the surface to show you what kind of spunk big Lake Trout have. Joe Loon goes off the beaten path where 4 and 5 lb. Brook Trout are caught with consistency. A fishing tale that fell prey to our cameras for all to enjoy.

Minipi Trout
Fly along in Lee Wulff's supercub as he and Curt Gowdy go in to fish untouched waters in the great Minipi Basin of Labrador. Lee discovered the most fabulous Brook Trout area of the Canadian north and took Curt in with him to share that miraculous fishing before it became known. You'll see big wild Brook Trout in flashing action.

Hit the High Trail to Adventure with: Curt Gowdy, Lee Wulff, Gene Hill, Jim Rikhoff and others.

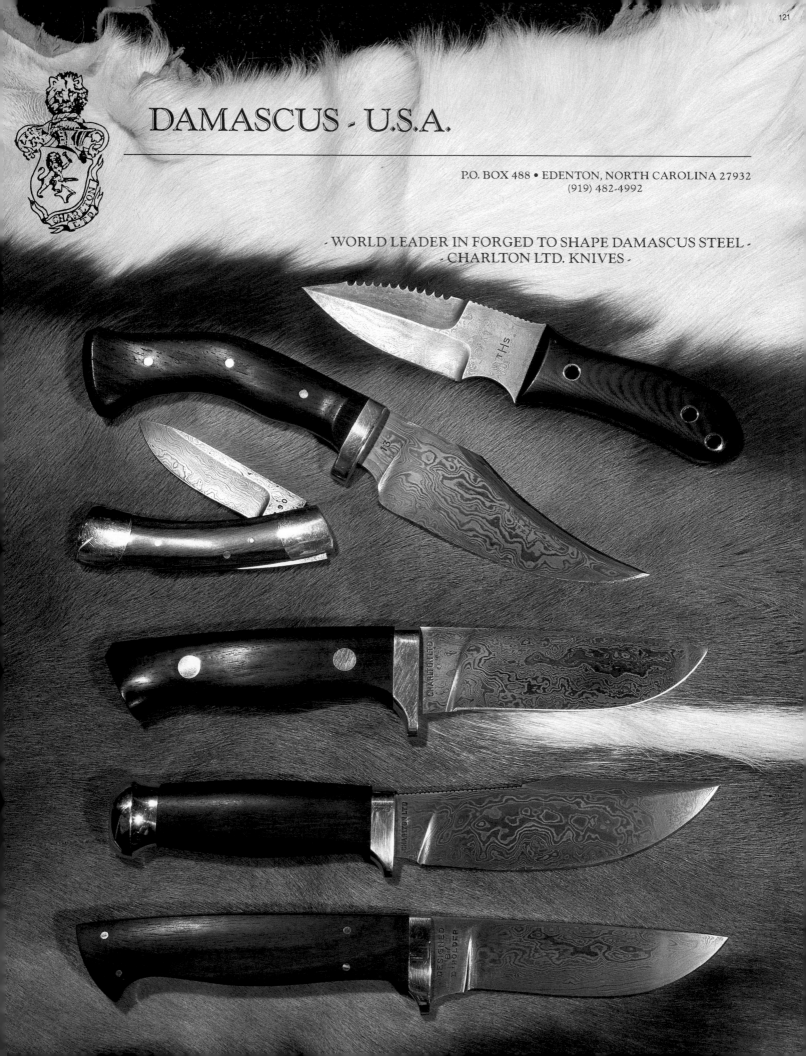

DAMASCUS - U.S.A.

P.O. BOX 488 • EDENTON, NORTH CAROLINA 27932
(919) 482-4992

· WORLD LEADER IN FORGED TO SHAPE DAMASCUS STEEL ·
· CHARLTON LTD. KNIVES ·

Alex J. Collins
K.K.K. Co.
Kustom Krafted Knives

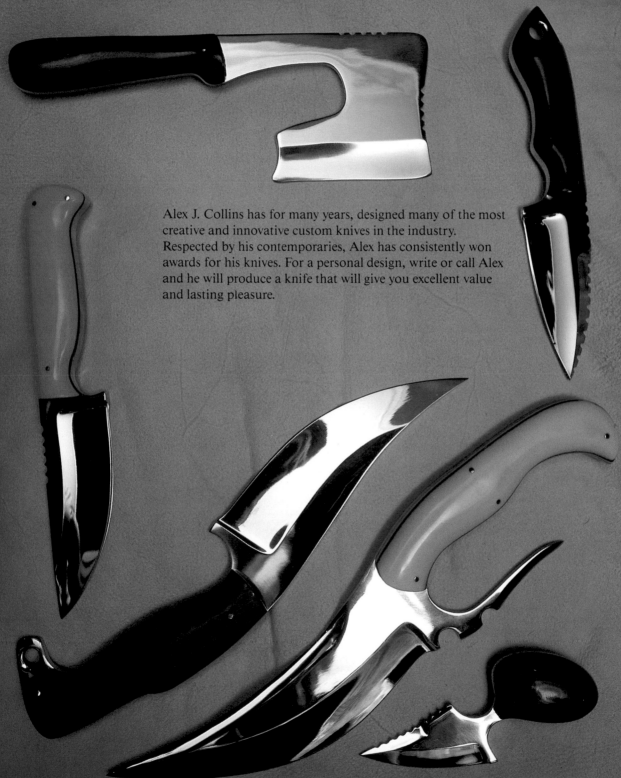

Alex J. Collins has for many years, designed many of the most creative and innovative custom knives in the industry. Respected by his contemporaries, Alex has consistently won awards for his knives. For a personal design, write or call Alex and he will produce a knife that will give you excellent value and lasting pleasure.

1834 W. Burbank Blvd.
Burbank, Calif. 91506
(818) 840-8400

Knives Designed
for Everyone
(818) 848-4905

CURRENT BOOKS IN PRINT

African Hunter by James Mellon
Regarded as the most comprehensive title ever on African hunting. There are fifty-two chapters on twenty countries and over 200 animals included in this large-format book. $105 — post paid

With a Rifle in Mongolia by Count Hoyos-Sprinzenstein
First English edition of the author's 1911 expedition to Mongolia and China. Limited to 500 numbered, slipcased copies. $85.00

White Hunter by John Hunter
Fine reprint of the first book ever written by the famous East African professional, John Hunter. Limited to 1,000 numbered, slipcased copies. $45.00

Horned Death by John Burger
Experiences of the famous John Burger who shot over 1,000 African buffalo during a lifetime of control hunting throughout Africa. Limited to 1,000 numbered, slipcased copies. $60.00

After Big Game in Central Africa by Eduoard Foa
Foa was a collector for the Paris National History Museum and hunted in what is, today, Tanzania and Zambia. Limited to 1,000 numbered, slipcased copies.
$75.00

Hunting on Three Continents with Jack O'Connor
by Jack O'Connor
A collection of stories — written during the period of 1973 to 1977 and covering his hunting adventures and experiences in North America, Africa and Asia. Title consists of entirely new material — never before published in book form. 2nd Edition $35.00
1st edition limited to 500 copies
signed by Bradford O'Connor. $45.00

From Mount Kenya to the Cape
by Craig Boddington
Boddington, Editor of Petersen's **Hunting** magazine, has gathered the experiences of some fourteen African hunts into this one volume. Spanning the last ten years, this book takes the reader from the slopes of Mt. Kenya to the wind-swept mountains of South Africa's Cape.
2nd edition $23.50
1st edition limited to 500 copies signed by author.$42.50

Books available directly from Safari Press, or from the specialist book dealers and better sporting goods stores.

Coming soon: **THE HUNTER IS DEATH** by T.V. Bulpin
HUNTING IN THE ROCKIES by Jack O'Connor.

To order: Send the price of the book   P&H ($2.00 per book) to Safari Press, P.O. Box 3095, Long Beach, CA 90803, USA. Please include a street address for UPS. VISA and MC accepted. Just call 213-430-3693 during business hours to order. CA res. add 6.5% tax.

ALL BOOKS SATISFACTION GUARANTEED OR YOUR MONEY BACK!

A postcard with your name and address will add you to our mailing list.

Finally!
THE
<u>*ULTIMATE*</u>
WORKING VEST FOR HUNTERS AND OBSERVERS

EASILY HOLDS
Raingear
Cartridges
Lunches
Scopes
Binoculars
Knife
Sunglasses
Baseball Cap
Gloves
Cameras
Film
Lenses

TO ORDER CONTACT:
Hunters Guide
25 MacDonald Ave.
Dartmouth, N.S.
Canada B3B 1C6
Tel. 902-468-2365
Fax 902-468-2236
or use the quick order form
in the back of the book.

VISIT OUR BOOTH AT SCI, WORLD CONGRESS AND FNAWS

HUNTERS • OUTFITTERS

DON'T MISS A SINGLE YEAR!

Subscribe now . . . and save

*FINALLY, A
SOURCE OF
OUTFITTERS &
SUPPLIERS IN
A PERMANENT
FORM.*

*HAVE THIS
BOOK SENT
TO YOU
DIRECTLY,
AS SOON
AS IT IS
PUBLISHED
EACH YEAR.*

SEE EASY SUBSCRIBER'S FORM AT THE BACK OF THE BOOK

Taxidermists Taxidermists
Taxidermists Taxidermists
Taxidermists Taxidermists
Taxidermists Taxidermists
Taxidermists Taxiderm
Taxidermists Taxider
Taxidermists Taxiderm
Taxidermists Taxidermi
Taxidermists Taxidermi
Taxidermists Taxidermi
Taxidermi

Taxidermists 8

The art of taxidermy is a craft few master. The taxidermist must have a keen sense of understanding regarding the actual animal or bird to be mounted.

We have a proven record of capturing the spirit of the subject and reflecting it in a finished product.

Taxidermy calls for a variety of skills. Our craftsmen sculpture mannequins, then stretch the hides upon them. We oil tan skins, taking 3 months to allow for best results and no cracking. These are just some of the things that add up to the perfect creation.

For the past 20 years, we have helped the autumn hunter and the serious safari gamesman alike.

We invite the local hunter to visit our facilities prior to going out on the hunt. Upon their visit, hunters will have the opportunity to view the care given to the ''prizes'' we create.

We know you respect and cherish the winged, webbed, and furred creatures of the wild. We give your trophy the same respect — taking the time necessary to create a quality masterwork.

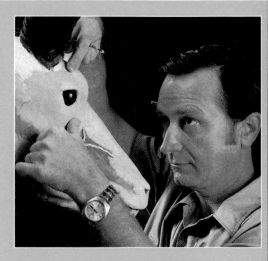

CONROE TAXIDERMY

Rt. 1, Box 282 AS
Conroe, Texas 77385

25908 I-45 N
Spring, Texas 77386

(713) 367-2745

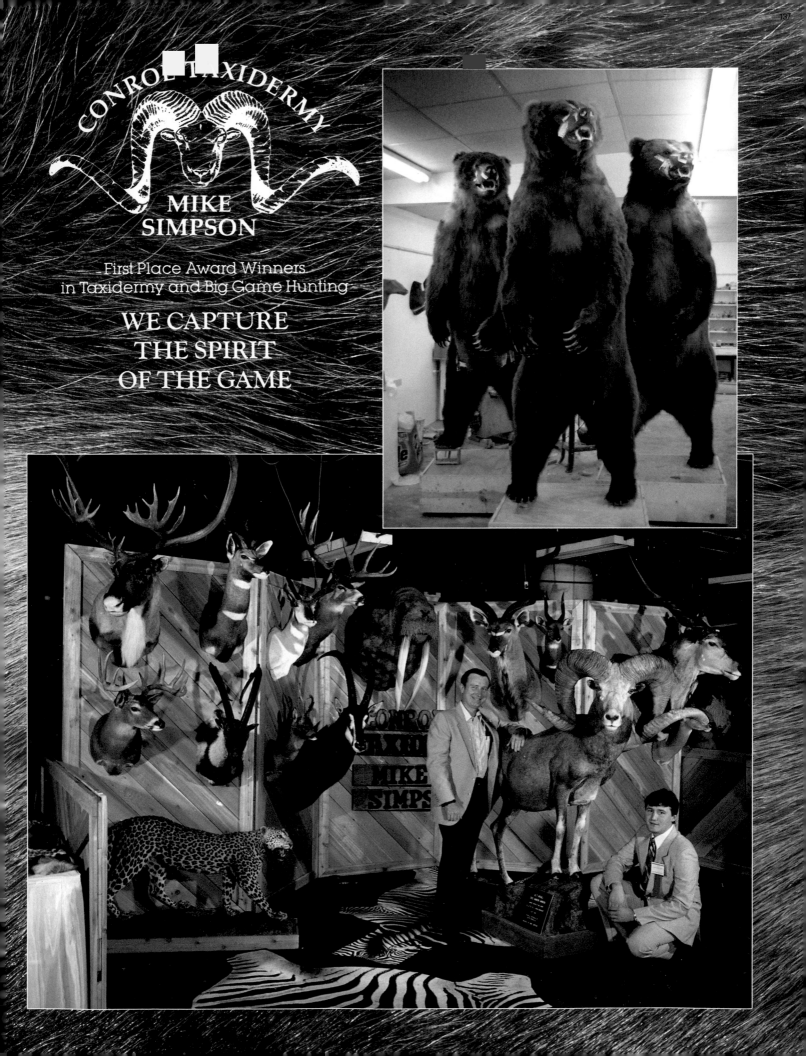

CONROE TAXIDERMY

MIKE SIMPSON

First Place Award Winners
in Taxidermy and Big Game Hunting

WE CAPTURE
THE SPIRIT
OF THE GAME

138

HeadsWest Taxidermy

4929 Ironton
Denver, Colorado 80239
(303) 371-8060

Capturing life in taxidermy

Uncommon animals from around the world are commonplace at HeadsWest. Record Book Trophies are entrusted to us and award winning mounts are returned in Record Time — while memories of the hunt are still fresh.

HeadsWest has in in house tannery whe trophies receive individual attention by hand and never leave the studio.

Serious Taxidermy for the (not always) Serious Hunter.

As a service to our clients HeadsWest will score trophies for Rowland Ward, Boone and Crockett, Pope and Young and Safari Club International.

HeadsWest's dedication to the sport of hunting comes from the belief that proper game management is essential. We will not accept endangered animals without a CITIES Permit from the county of origin. Proof that the animal was legally taken is required for all protected animals.

HeadsWest Taxidermy

929 Ironton
Denver, Colorado 80239
(303) 371-8060

Capturing life in taxidermy

For over 15 years HeadsWest
has welcomed the challenge of
custom Taxidermy for private
collections and public museums.

HeadsWest has won awards in
major national Taxidermy
competitions, but the amount of
repeat business we get from
trophy hunters is the best
evidence of the quality of
our work.

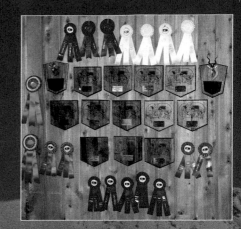

The serious collector is the best judge of the quality of
our work, that is why so many record book trophies are
mounted by HeadsWest.

GAME BIRDS · RUGS · TROPHY FISH

SACKVILLE TAXIDERMY
997 SACKVILLE DR., LOWER SACKVILLE
NOVA SCOTIA, CANADA B4E 1S3

Notes

Artists Artists
Artists Artists
Artists Artists
Artists Artists
Artists Artists
Artists Artists
Artists Artists
Artists Artists

Artists 9

Artists Artists

Being a hunter and outdoorsman, I have always been inspired by the beauty of nature and have tried to capture this in my subjects and material.

Dan Bridge
Box 16, Site 8 Airport
RR #1, Fort St. John
British Columbia, Canada V1J 4M6
604-785-5522

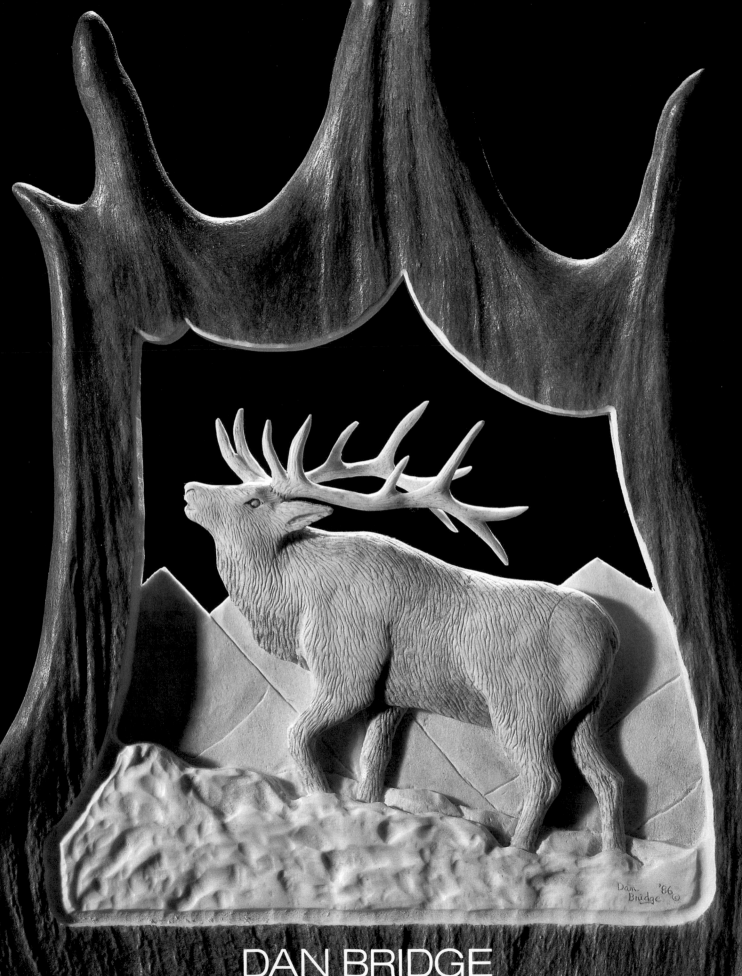

DAN BRIDGE
A PIECE OF THE OUTDOORS

*William M. Davis —
Specializing in North American
big game and game birds in
bronze. In recent years some
western pieces have been
executed. Extreme detail
unsurpassed in the bronze field
is his hallmark.*

*Bill has participated in many
western competitions such as
the Audubon shows and the
Buffalo Bill Western Art Show.*

*His work is in many prominent
collections such as Gene Autry,
Burt Reynolds, Governor
Dukemejian of California and
President Ronald Reagan.*

*Bill resides in Wapiti Valley just
30 miles from the east entrance
to Yellowstone Park.*

Title: 7 and 7
Size: 18" x 30"
Edition: 25

Title: On the Rims
Size: 18" x 30"
Edition: 25

WILLIAM
DAVIS

LIMITED EDITION BRONZES
AND WATERCOLORS

P.O. BOX 50
WAPITI, WYOMING 82450
(307) 527-7634

The Bronzes of . . .
Lorenzo Ghiglieri

*Eloquent, strong and original.
Already, people from all over the
world are excited about owning
his works and enthused about
being part of a career that is
growing rapidly. Lorenzo has
created over 200 different themes
on American and Canadian culture,
historical events and wildlife.
We show here just a glimpse of this
master's works. There is in his art
an inspiration with universal appeal
that has meaning and purpose.
The message rings clear . . .
It is powerful, it is valuable, it is
beautiful and it is American . . .*

BRUTE FORCE (17″ x 11″)
*available in bronze or
pure .999 silver.*

Available at . . .
LORENZO'S STUDIO
995 S.W. Highland Drive
Gresham, OR 97080 (563) 667-7776

The Bronzes of...
Lorenzo Ghiglieri

*Eloquent, strong and original.
Already, people from all over the
world are excited about owning
his works and enthused about
being part of a career that is
growing rapidly. Lorenzo has
created over 200 different themes
on American and Canadian culture,
historical events and wildlife.
We show here just a glimpse of this
master's works. There is in his art
an inspiration with universal appeal
that has meaning and purpose.
The message rings clear...
It is powerful, it is valuable, it is
beautiful and it is American...
Join his quest.*

Rat's End'' (20"x17")

Lorenzo E. Ghiglieri Inc., **995 S.W. Highland Drive, Gresham, Oregon 97030 (503) 667-7776 (503) 665-4993**

Whether you're an investor, a serious collector, or simply a lover of fine sculpture or colorful paintings, Lee has a variety of subjects and sizes to choose from.

If there is a specific work of art you seek regarding wildlife or the West, Lee would be happy to work with you on a commission basis, please call or write.

Title — Rocky Mountain Royalty   Edition — 20
Size — 27" high, 29" long

Title — Caught by Surprise   Edition — 20
Size — 12" high, 19" long

Title — Autumn Gold   Edition — 20
Size — 16" high, 32" long

Title — Efforts Paid Off
Edition — 50
Size 18" high, 10" round

Title — Summer Run
Edition — 20
Size — 11" high, 15" long

Title: Silent Partner
Edition — 20
Size 14" high, 15" long

Box 534 • Joseph, Oregon 97846 • (503) 432-8795

DENNIS JONES

Dennis Jones has quickly earned a national reputation as one of the most premiere wildlife artists in America today. His skills have conveyed the power and beauty of wildlife around the world. "I try to make my work appear as if there is something going on outside the bronze itself. Each piece of art seems to draw your imagination away from the sculpture to a place or time that each of us as outdoorsmen have experienced."

Low editions, fine detail, powerful compositions and a high regard for accuracy make Dennis' bronzes a fine investment. Collectors and sportsmen from across the country have appreciated more the beauty of our wildlife heritage through the efforts of Dennis Jones.

Khayam, the 1½ lifesize bronze (above) was a project Dennis was commissioned by the city of Winston, Oregon and the Wildlife Safari to commemorate this beautiful animal. The cheetah truly is an investment worth considering.

Title — Survival on the Serengeti   Edition — 10   Size — 18″ high, 31″ high

Survival on the Serengeti portrays the beauty, power and elegance of this magnificent creature. The fastest animal on earth, the cheetah, is definitely an animal worthy of our appreciation.

DESIREE DAWN
ARTIST

RT#1, BOX 407
JOSEPH, OR. 97846
503•432•9235

ON THE ALERT
Desiree Dawn

Notes

Travel & Airlines

Airlines & Travel 10

THE ALL-AROUND CANADIAN

Some of Canada's coldest country boasts some of Canada's warmest people. But warmth is what the Canadian spirit is all about. It's what we offer travellers from coast to coast in the Canadian Arctic. Warm, friendly service. Convenient, reliable schedules. In Whitehorse, Inuvik and Iqaluit (Frobisher Bay). And a lot of places in between.

Furthermore, if you're seeking the warmth of the Canadian South, it's good to know that Canadian Airlines serves all major cities here at home from coast to coast, including Montréal, Toronto, Calgary and Vancouver. Of course, we also fly further afield. In fact we serve more destinations on five continents than any other airline in Canada.

If the idea of travelling makes you warm all over, think Canadian.

THE SPIRIT TAKES WING.
Canadian Airlines International

Go places with Dan-Air from Scotland

DAN-AIR LONDON

Many people know that Dan-Air have grown to be one of the leading scheduled airlines in Britain.

Operating regular scheduled flights to 28 destinations in Britain, Ireland and mainland Europe.

Smooth, comfortable travel on our modern aircraft including on some routes the new British BAe 146 jetliner.

Good food and drink, with full meals on longer flights.

And a standard of service Dan-Air's famous competitors find hard to match.

So whether you travel on business or for pleasure, fly Dan-Air Scheduled Services from Scotland.

Phone your travel agent or call Dan-Air direct on (0463) 226349.

INVERNESS
ABERDEEN
NEWCASTLE
LONDON HEATHROW
LONDON GATWICK

DAN✈AIR
SCHEDULED SERVICES
We're going places

Look who's making a new name for themselves on the Atlantic.

Northwest. A new name, a bigger airline. Now we put over 300 modern jetliners at your service, flying to over 130 cities in 19 countries in 3 continents.

A new name. But an established reputation as the fastest-growing Transatlantic airline. And over 60 years' experience since we started operation as one of the USA's pioneer airlines.

A new name. And a new resolve to give still higher standards of service, still better value for money.

See for yourselves when you fly between Boston or New York and Glasgow Prestwick on our superb 747s – the only direct scheduled services between the United States and Scotland.

A new name. And now, through Boston or New York, we can offer connections by our domestic flights or by Northwest Airlink services between almost 200 US cities and Scotland.

For reservations, see your travel agent or contact your nearest Northwest office.

Look to us.

NORTHWEST

Scottish Highlands

Set in three acres of woodland and gardens, only one mile south of the centre of town, this lovely converted 18th century mansion reflects the unhurried atmosphere of days gone by, yet combines truly high standards of cuisine and modern comforts with friendly, personal service. Our 54 bedrooms have private bathrooms, colour television, telephones and radio, and offer the choice of luxury bed sittingrooms, family rooms, separate golf villas, really superb 'doubles' and very well appointed twin and single bedded rooms. Private Squash Courts and adjacent to the fine 18 hole Inverness Golf Course.

Please write for our brochure and tariff, or phone us at 0463 237166.

A.A. ✱✱✱   Egon Ronay

KINGSMILLS HOTEL

Culcabock Road, Inverness, Scotland IV2 3LP. Telephone: (0463) 237166. Telex: 75566.

In the heart of the Scottish Borders, set in 200 acres of woodland and gardens on the banks of the river Teviot, is Sunlaws House Hotel. Owned by the Duke and Duchess of Roxburghe, this charming converted country gentlemens retreat reflects an atmosphere of times past, yet offers a truly high standard of cuisine and modern comfort with friendly and distinctive service.

All 21 bedrooms have private bathroom, colour television, radio and direct dial telephone.

Sunlaws is an ideal retreat, whether for a private holiday, board meeting or a sporting-break.

Situated 5 minutes drive from Kelso it is the perfect location for touring the Borders. Kelso, Dryburgh and Sweetheart Abbeys are all nearby as is Abbotsford, the home of Sir Walter Scott. Great Houses such as Mellerstain, Bowhill and Floors Castle are within minutes from Sunlaws too.

Many of our guests are sportsmen fishing for salmon on the Tweed or our private beats of the Teviot or alternatively fishing for trout from our fully stocked lake next to the hotel. Many come to shoot on the great estates nearby.

Our close connections with Roxburghe Estates has given us a professionalism with sporting events that is second to none and this can clearly be seen in the exciting and growing sport of clay pigeon shooting which we have in the grounds. All standards are catered for, from beginners to the more proficient shot, in a varied and challenging layout with stands simulating driven grouse, high pheasant, duck flighting and bolting rabbit with full instruction given by the estates expert team. This is an unusual and enjoyable way of business entertaining and is available to private parties or to companies.

Nearby is Floors Castle, the home of the present Duke and Duchess of Roxburghe, overlooking the river Tweed it occupies one of the most beautiful sites in Scotland. For guests at Sunlaws special tours can be arranged by private arrangement prior to arriving at the hotel.

For further information or a brochure of Sunlaws House Hotel and its facilities write to David J. Corkill or telephone him on 05735 331.

Sunlaws House Hotel
Kelso Roxburghshire
TD5 8JZ Scotland

Telex: 728147 SUNLAW G
Telephone: 05735 331
USA: 800-323-5463

Bear shot placement

text and drawings by Erik van Veenen

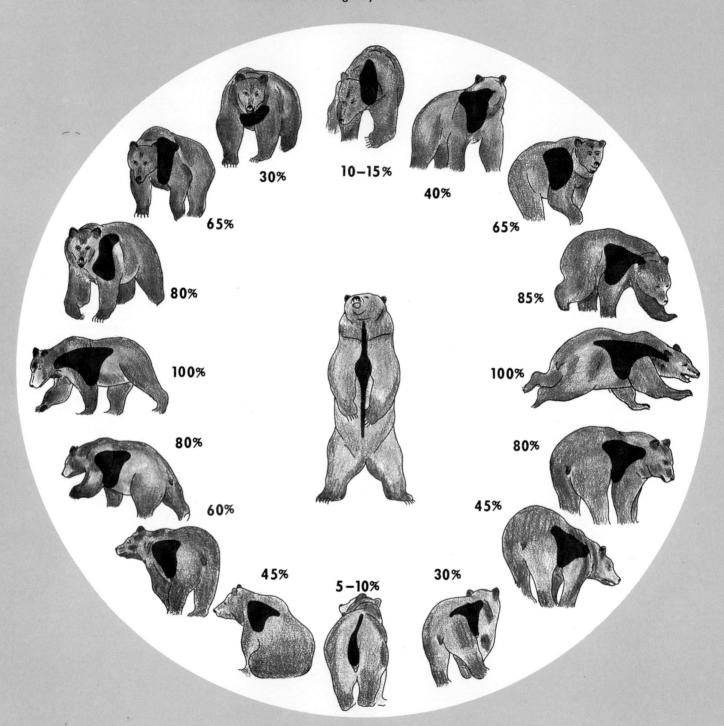

30% · 10–15% · 40% · 65% · 65% · 80% · 85% · 100% · 100% · 80% · 80% · 45% · 60% · 45% · 5–10% · 30%

Shooting angles

The figure next to the Bear indicates roughly the amount of vital area exposed at various angles.

Exposure of vital areas depends on the angle at which the Bear is turned toward the hunter. Broadside is the best possible angle with most (100%) of vital area exposed. <u>Aim at the center of the shoulder!</u>

A Bear walking away at an angle will show only 80% to 45% of the vital area. A Bear pointing straight away from the hunter will show only 5% vital area, and presents the least desirable shooting angle. A Bear running broadside past the hunter will expose nearly 100% vital area but is a very difficult shot requiring a lead depending on the speed and distance of the animal.

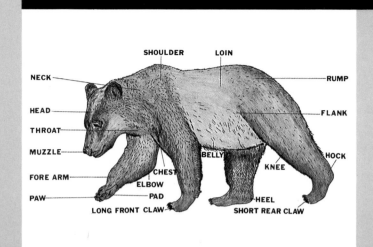

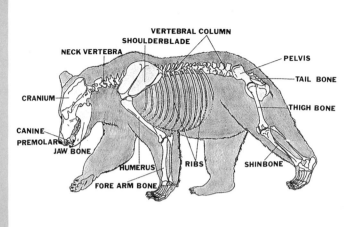

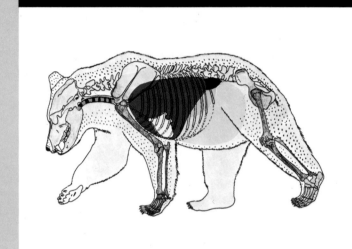

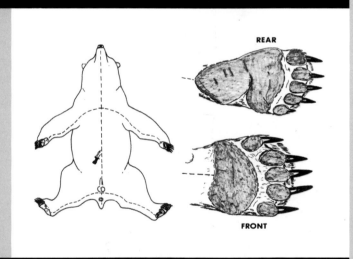

Shoulder shot: chest cavity, heart, lungs, sure death, dispatch quickly.

Gutshot: escape and slow death if not followed up.

Kidneys: vital area, will die if not followed up.

Liver: serious wound, likely to die if not followed up.

Esophagus and jugular vein: will bleed or starve to death.

Flesh or muscular wounds: may permanently cripple.

Structural damage: crippling, often impeded after recovery.

Central nervous system: head, neck, spine; Bear will likely stay down, escape if only partially paralyzed.

Trophy care

Make cuts as straight as possible to obtain a symmetrical rug.

Remove all fat and flesh and split the ears, lips, nose and tail before salting.

Pay special attention to the feet by removing bones and fat to the first (claw) joint.

Don't expose the stretched hide to direct sunlight, let dry in the shade. Salt entire rug heavily.

Outfitters Outf
Directory Directory
Outfitters Outfitter
Directory Direct
Outfitters Outfit
Directory Direct
Outfitters Outl
Directory Dire
Outfitters Out
Directory Dir

Outfitters Directory 11

Outfitters Directory: Hunting

Africa

Botswana

Association of Hunting
Safari Operators
Box 119
Maun
Botswana

McFarlane, R.
Box 1602
Gaborone
Botswana

Vira Safaris Ltd.
P.O. Box 1602
Gaborne
Botswana
372308

Roussos, Nassos
Guide/Outfitter
Box 3658
Addis Ababa
Ethiopia

Namibia

Mount Etjo Safari Lodge
P.O. Box 81
Kalkfeld 9000
Namibia
06532-1602
Mr. J. Oelofse

Trophyland Safaris
Box 37
Rundu
Namibia
016-401016
Mr. F. Bartlett

South Africa

3 B Ranch
Elysium
P.O. Kiesel 0382
South Africa
015379-921
Mr. D.G. Bubb

AAA Hunting
P.O. Box 4789
Pretoria 0001
South Africa

African Safaris Unlimited
Box 41332
Craighall
South Africa 2024
011-880-1948
Mr. J. Brelsford

Ameland Safaris
P.O. Box 241
Potgietesus
South Africa 0600
Mr. C. van der Merwe

Angus Brown Safaris
Box 666
Ellisras
South Africa 0555
015362 AskFor 2912
Mr. A. Brown

Answa Safaris
Box 542
Silverton 0127
South Africa
012-862312
Mr. J. Swart

Ayliffe, Lance
26 Mackeurtan Ave.
Durban North
South Africa 4051
031-847815
Mr. L. Ayliffe

Baobab Safaris
P.O. Box 512
Potgietersrus 0600
South Africa
015332-830
Mr. J. Schoeman

Basie Maartens
Mountain Shadows
Box 2501
Paarl 7620
South Africa
02211-623192

Beck, L.R.
Box 91252
Auckland Park 2006
South Africa

Belvedere Safaris
P.O. Box 84
Bedford 5780
South Africa
04632-2522
1120 Bedford
Willem de Klerk or Noel Ross

Berry, Mark
Box 616
Kimberley 8300
South Africa
0531-22919

Biggs, Russell
Pioneers Park
Box 30124
Windhoek 9000
South Africa
061-41665

Bivack Game Ranch
Box 61
Alldays 0909
South Africa
01554-360
Mr. H.G. Wollert

Bonamanzi Game Ranches
P.O. Box 48
Hluhluwe 3960
South Africa
Code 03562 Ask For
3530 Or 143 A.H.
Nigel Fairhead or Martin
Brammer

Botha, Christo
Box 727
Potgietersrus 0600
South Africa
01541-4710

Bowker & Scott Safaris
Box 80
Tarkastad
South Africa
Mr. F. Bowker

Bowker, Francis
Box 442
Grahamstown 6140
South Africa
0461-5203

Buffalo Safaris
P.O. Box 29050
Sunnyside 0132
South Africa
012-465327
Mr. Kobus Prinsloo

Buffalo Safaris
Box 26292
Arcadia 0007
South Africa
012-465327
Maj.Gen. Minnaar

Calverley, Mark
P/Bag X070145
Wasbank 2920
South Africa

Outfitters Directory: Hunting

Africa

Carlstein, K.M.
32 St. Johns Wood
Boeing Road
Bedfordview 2008
South Africa

Cawood, Michael
Gannahoek
Box 12
Mortimer 5870
South Africa
0486-606

Coenraad Vermaak Safaris
Box 739
Dundee 3000
South Africa
03425-729
Mr. D.A. Beattie

Confederation of
Hunters Associations
Box 911-217
Rosslyn 0200
South Africa

Costhuizen, John C.
P/Bag X071
Marshalltown 2107
South Africa
011-836-6525

D'Alton, M.J.
Box 400
Bredasdorp 7280
South Africa
0284-42142

Daly, Bill
Box 4974
Durban 4000
South Africa
031-313985

de Bruijn, Lud
Box 115
Somerset East 5850
South Africa
042412-1820

Deane, Robert C.
Box 79
Hluhluwe 3960
South Africa
03562 Ask For 144

Dedekind, Ernst
Safaris
P.O. Box 14
Moolman 2387
South Africa

Dippenaar, C.R.
Box 1057
Nelspruit 1200
South Africa
01311-22367

Du Plessis, K.A.
Faunafrika
Box 53
Vaalwater 0530
South Africa
015236-5702

East Cape Game
Management Association
Box 1059
Queenstown 5320
South Africa

Ellington Ranch
P.O. Box 207
Ellisras 0555
South Africa
Mr. A. Brown

Erasmus, Willem P.
Box 1414
Kempton Park 1620
South Africa

Esser, Franz J.
40 Morsim Road
Hyde Park 2196
South Africa

Executive Safaris
Box 12614
Clubview 0014
South Africa

Faunafrika
P.O. Box 53
Vaalwater 0530
South Africa
27-11-683-4350

Flanagan, Marge
Box 1510
Honeydew 2040
South Africa
011-795-2133

Free State Safaris
P.O. Box 7
Kroonstad 9500
South Africa
01411-23468
Mr. Theo Erasmus

Frylinck, Athol
Box 1822
Vryburg 8600
South Africa
01451-4141

G. G. Viglietti
42 Caxton Way
Oakridge 7800
South Africa
015352-144
Mr. L.J.C. Van Tonder

Game Bird Safaris
Box 299
Vryheid 3100
South Africa
0386-667
Mr. T.D. Comins

Ghenzi, C.A.
Box 69748
Bryanston 2021
South Africa
011-7043060

Giulietti, F.
Box 232
Paulshof 2056
South Africa

Goss, Ian L.
Box 10
Magudu 3160
South Africa
038292 AskFor 2130

Greater Kuduland Safaris
Box 115
Tshipise 0901
South Africa
015539-920
Mr. B.W. Van Wulfften Palthe

Greer, Graham W.
Box 403
Paulshof 2056
South Africa

Grobler, Donald K.
10 Ruthleigh Drive
Westville 3630
South Africa
031-821504

Guillaume, Bertie & Celia
Box 733
Louis Trichardt 0920
South Africa
01551-9762

Outfitters Directory: Hunting

Africa

Halse, A.R.D.
Box 9
Sterkstroom 4025
South Africa
04592-3311

Hannan, Edward A.D.
P/Bag X527
Mkuze 3965
South Africa
03562 Ask For
Mkuze 1931

Harmse, Frans
Box 4124
Germiston South 1411
South Africa

Harmse, Neil
Box 407
Malelane 1320
South Africa
0131622-144

Haselau, G.R.
Box 2501
Paarl 7620
South Africa

Havemann, Louis J.
P.O. Heatonville
Windy Ridge 3881
South Africa
0351-23465

Henderson, Ian M.
Box 6
Knysna 6570
South Africa
0445-22894

Hiles, Roland
Box 2269
Beacon Bay 5205
South Africa

Hockley, Robin
Cullendale
Bedford 5780
South Africa
04632-1303

Holbrow, Peter J.
11 Surrey Lane
Kloof 3600
South Africa
031-741137

Hongony Hunting Safaris
Box 18
Klaserie 1381
South Africa
0131732-2802
Mr. G.P. Van Niekerk

Ingwe Safaris
Box 218
Hoedspruit 1380
South Africa
0131732-3304
Mr. K.A. McCarter

Ingwe Safaris
Box 218
Hoedspruit 1380
South Africa
0020 Ask For
MICA 803
Mr. T. Otto

Inkasa Safaris
Box 13876
Northmead 1511
South Africa
011-849-2082
Mr. A. Grobbelaar

Inter-Africa Safaris
Pty. Ltd.
Box 72
Klaserie 1381
South Africa
0131732-2423
Mr. P. Otto

Intergame Africa
Property Ltd.
Box 78495
Sandton 2146
South Africa

Jackson, Timothy N.S.
Box 91229
Auckland Park 2006
South Africa
011-726-6803

Johnson, P.G.
Box 460
Bergvlei 2012
South Africa

Jones, P.A.
Box 72
Muldersdrift 1747
South Africa

Joubert, Hendrik P.
Box 578
Germiston 1400
South Africa
011-8270970

Karise Farm & Pheasantry
Box 121
Eikenhof 1872
South Africa
011-948-9739
Mr. E.J. Pittaway

Kelly, Garry
11 Surrey Lane
Kloof 3600
South Africa
031-741137

Kelly, John W.
19 Homeford Drive
La Lucia 4051
South Africa
031-525942

Kido Safaris
P.O. Box 511
Pretoria 0001
South Africa
2712-46-3156
Mr. P. Pienaar

Knott, Peter and Howard
Box 1385
Louis Trichardt 0920
South Africa
01551-9663

Knowles, J.G.
c/o Box 106
Letsitele 0885
South Africa
0152332-2321

Kohrs, Karl
P/Bag X516
Mkuze 3965
South Africa
03562 Ask For
Mkuze 1303

Lamprecht, J.J.
Box 305
Ellisras 0555
South Africa

Limpopo Hunting Safaris
Box 431
Howick 3290
South Africa
03324-4525
Mr. J.R. Coleman

Outfitters Directory: Hunting

Africa

Lindsay, Donald C.
Box 227
Vanderbijlpark 1900
South Africa
01617-330

Loubser Safaris
Box 538
Thabazimbi 0380
South Africa
619-356-1700
Mr. L. Bornt

Loubser Safaris Africa
Box 12026
Cape Town 8000
South Africa
Mr. Francois Loubser

Loubser, Francois
Box 538
Thabazimbi 0380
South Africa
015379-607

Louw, Gerrit J.R.
Box 494
Thabazimbi 0380
South Africa
015379 AskFor82630

Magnum Hunting Safaris
Box 611
Louis Trichardt 0920
South Africa
01551-4069

Manning, Jack
Box 5
Mkuze 3965
South Africa
03562 Ask For 2831

Marais, Dr. J.T.
Box 2693
Pretoria 0001
South Africa
012-215957

Marais, J.D.
Exclusive Safaris
Box 833
Krugersdorp 1740
South Africa
011-6699834

McDonald Wildlife
Property Ltd.
Box 37
Tshipise 0901
South Africa
015539-719
Mr. Sandy McDonald

McNeil, Hugh A.
Box 893
Johannesburg 2000
South Africa
011-613-6777

Miles, Paul H.A.
c/o Box 115
Somerset East 5850
South Africa

Millican, R.R.
Box 128
Stanger 4450
South Africa
0324-21288

Mkuze Falls Safaris
Box 236
Pongola 3170
South Africa
03841-31560
Mr. E. Bouwer

Mkuze Falls Safaris
Box 248
Pongola 3170
South Africa
038422-1604
Mr. A.J. Marais

Mmabolela Safaries
P.O. Box 29
Swartwater 0622
South Africa
015432 ask for
Masstown 704
Mr. J. Van Der Meulen

Mountain View Farm
Klipfontein
Lydenburg 1120
South Africa
Mr. A. de Jager

Mulobezi Safaris
P.O. Box 7468
Petic 1512
South Africa
Mr. A. McCallum

Murray, W.S.
Box 237
Graaff Reinet 6280
South Africa

Natal Hunters and
Game Conservation Assoc.
Box 4974
Durban 4000
South Africa

North-Western Safaris
P.O. Box 21
Swartwater 0622
South Africa
Mr. D. Van Der Meulen

North-Western Safaris
Box 328
Johannesburg 2000
South Africa
011-609-6808
011-838-2405
Mr. I. Ritchie

Nyala Game Ranch
Box 73
Kwambonambi 3915
South Africa
0352-876
Mr. R. Barnes

Nyalaveld Safaris
Box 87
Mkuze 3965
South Africa
03562 Ask For
Mkuze 1931
Mr. T. Irwin

Nyalaveld Safaris
Pty. Ltd.
Box 3741
Durban 4000
South Africa
031-313403

Palala Safaris
P.O. Box 191
Silverton 0127
South Africa
Mr. C.W.M. du Toit

Pallamar, Werner A.
Box 781038
Sandton 2146
South Africa
011-84-1327

Parkes, James
Box 184
Graaff Reinet 6280
South Africa
0491-23078

Peens, J.A.
Box 310
Potgietersrus 0600
South Africa

Outfitters Directory: Hunting

Africa

Pro Nobis Hunting Safaris
Box 5
Hluhluwe 3960
South Africa
03562 Ask For 5
Mr. A. Meintjes

Rand Arms & Safaris Pty.
Marlborough House
60 Eloff Street
Johannesburg 2001
South Africa
011-3315180
Mr. C.D. Smith

Ras, M.D.
Tsuma Putego
Box 179
Thabazimbi 0380
South Africa
015379-724

Rautenbach, Sigi
Lakefield Ext. 21
85 Torquay St.
Benoni 1500
South Africa
011-8941966

Reinstorf, S.C.
Box 484
Piet Retief 2380
South Africa

Rooipoort Safaris
Box 616
Kimberley 8300
South Africa
0531-22915
Mr. A.J. Anthony

Roos, Peter C.
Box 276
Kroondal 0350
South Africa

Roux, Daniel F.
Box 4443
Pretoria 0001
South Africa

Rowland Ward SA Pty. Ltd.
CC Box 99-142
Carlton Centre
Johannesburg 2001
South Africa
011-3315410

Rudling, Tony
Box 383
Alberton 1450
South Africa
011-3391814

SA Bowhunting and
Game Conservation Assoc.
438 King's Highway
Lynwood 0081
South Africa

SA Tourism and
Safari Association
41 Rustenburg Rd.
Melville 2092
South Africa
011-726-7763

Sabi Sabi
Box 1170
Johannesburg 2000
South Africa
011-833-7481

Schimper, Frank
Box 343
Krugersdorp 1740
South Africa
011-763-3851

Scott, William H.
Box 80
Tarkastad 5371
South Africa
04582-4202

Seegers, Jaap
Box 343
Vaalwater 0530
South Africa
015352 Ask For 96

Shepherd, Grant
Box 78
Klaserie 1381
South Africa

Sinclair, C.A.
Box 135
Louis Trichardt 0920
South Africa

Skuilkrans Safaris
P.O. Box 73008
Fairland 2030
South Africa
Mr. F. Hartzer

Smith, Stephen J.
105 Athol Rd.
Atholl 2199
South Africa
011-783-5012

Sparks, Chappie
Box 557
Queenstown 5320
South Africa
0451-2325

Sparrow, Ronnie
Box 381
Muldersdrift 1747
South Africa
011-666-2507

Stegmann, W.A.
River Villa w/s 404
Bourkestraat 71
Sunnyside 0002
South Africa

Sussens, C.G.
Box 289
Hoedspruit 1380
South Africa

Swanepoel, J.H.
Box 49
Hartbeespoort 0216
South Africa
01211-31975

Swart, J.G.
Box 538
Thabazimbi 0380
South Africa

The Transvaal
Game Association
Box 2603
Pretoria 0001
South Africa

Theron, A.M.
24 Stratton Ave.
Bryanston 2021
South Africa

Theron, P.A.
149 Wilton Ave.
Bryanston 2021
South Africa

Thomas, K.D.
Box 1424
Queenstown 5320
South Africa

Thring, Brian
Box 102
Hluhluwe 3960
South Africa

Outfitters Directory: Hunting

Africa

Tinley, Charles
Box 87
Tarkastad 5370
South Africa
04582-5402

Tomkinson, A.J.
Box 657
Greytown 3500
South Africa

Tonks, Lewes
Camdeboo Safaris
Box 427
Graaff Reinet 6280
South Africa
23038

Tout, Mark
Box 20
Mica 1380
South Africa

Trophyland Safaris
Box 7611
Johannesburg 2000
South Africa
011-838-4235

Tsolwana Game Ranch
Box 87
Tarkastad 5370
South Africa
04582-5211

Van Coppenhagen, Lou
Box 29144
Sunnyside 0231
South Africa
012-346-1135

Van Den Heever, Daan
Tumuga Safaris
Box 1427
Potgietersrus 0600
South Africa
01541-5254

Van Der Merwe, C.J.
Box 241
Potgietersrus 0600
South Africa
01541-2710

Van Der Post, Alec
Box 35415
Northcliff 2115
South Africa
011-678-1603

Van Graan, Daniel J.
Engonyameni Safaris
Box 9
Kaapmuiden 1295
South Africa
1621

Van Greunen, Faan
P/Bag 2471
Potgietersrus 0600
South Africa

Van Rooyen, Johann
Box 3789
Pietersburg 0700
South Africa
01521-6379

Van Rooyen, Nico
Box 217
Rosslyn 0200
South Africa
012-582126

Van Straten, C.J.
35 Second Road
Linbro Park 2199
South Africa

Van Tonder, L.J.C.
Box 375
Vaalwater 0530
South Africa
015352-144

Vermaak, Audley G.
P.O. Glenconnor 6234

South Africa
041-28259

Vimercati, Paulo
Box 372
Honeydew 2040
South Africa
011-660-5640

Vira Safaris
P/Bag 1046
Waterpoort 0905
South Africa
Mr. I.B. McFarlane

Vivier, Johny
Box 248
Pongola 3170
South Africa

Wagendrift Safaris
Box 463
Piet Retief 2380
South Africa
27-13431-860
Mr. C. Labuschagne

Wagendrift Safaris
P.O. Box 463
Piet Retief 2380
South Africa
013431-860
Mr. C.S. Labuschagne

Waring, Neil
Box 54
Mkuze 3965
South Africa

Wex, C.I.
Box 619
Umtentweni 4235
South Africa
0391-21768

Wildlife Expeditions
P.O. Box 645
Bedfordview 2008
South Africa
011-53-1814
011-53-8411
Mr. C. Walker

Wildlife Society of SA
Box 44189
Linden 2104
South Africa

Wildspan Hunting
Box 5
Campbell 8360
South Africa
0020 Ask For
Campbell 1330
Mr. Hendrik Van Eck

Wilkinson, Chris
12 York Rd.
Gillitts 3610
South Africa
0381-4861

World Expedition & Safari
Box 11450
Secunda 2302
South Africa
011-27-13-6344379
Mr. A. Hattingh

Young, Dr. Eddie
Box 60
Swartklip 0370
South Africa

Zingela Safaris
P.O. Box 1057
Nelspruit 1200
South Africa
Mr. T. Shaw

Outfitters Directory: Hunting

Africa

Zulu Bush Safaris
Box 832
Vryheid 3100
South Africa
0381-4861
Mr. D.J. Paul

Zulu Nyala Safaris
P.O. Box 1775
Johannesburg 2000
South Africa
011-27-11-290898
Mr. T. Shaw

Hunting Africa #111
P.O. Box 30573
Sunnyside 0132
South Africa
Mr. F. Basson

Kgama Safaris
Box 1201
Mogwase 0302
Bophuthatswana
South Africa
014292-2405

Engonyameni Safaris
Box 9
Kaapmuiden 1295 East.
Transvaal
South Africa
Mr. D. Van Graan

Cat Pardo
P.O. Box 2
Alldays N. Transvaal
South Africa
Mr. D. Uys

Cormack, Gordon
Professional Hunter
251 Boshoff St.
Pietermaritzburg Natal 3201
South Africa

Kliphoek Lodge
Palala Safaris
6 Tomkordale Building
Dekgras Street Silvertondale
South Africa
86-8005,86-8016
86-8022,86-4848

Chete Safaris
Box 10442
Aston Manor 1630 Transvaal
South Africa
011-964-1025
Mr. F. Rademeyer

Zambia

Big Game Safaris
P.O. Box 35813
Lusaka
Zambia
Mr. G. Raftopoulos

Busanga Trails
P.O. Box 31322
Lusaka
Zambia
216715
Mr. D.H. Price

Higgins, Darryl M.
Box 30675
Lusaka
Zambia

International Safaris
P.O. Box 35813
Luska
Zambia
Mr. Geoff Broom

Kazuma Safaris Ltd.
P.O. Box 330793
Lusaka
Zambia
Mr. P. Swanepoel

Professional Hunters
Association of Zambia
Box 10
Chisamba
Zambia

United Safaris, Ltd.
P.O. Box 35370
Lusaka
Zambia
Mr. J. Chalansi

Zimbabwe

Baird, James
Diamond Ranch
Box 18
Kudoma
Zimbabwe
Munyati 2424
219-464-8216 USA

**Hunters Tracks
(Private) Ltd.
P.O. Box CH 4
Chisipite
Zimbabwe
736797 Harare
329 Arcturus**

Nuanetsi Hunters
P. Bag 2008
Mwenezi
Zimbabwe
Mr. Don Price

Rosslyn Safaris
Pvt. Bag 5934
Hwange
Zimbabwe
Hwange 70223

Vadoma Safaris
Box 296
Kwe Kwe
Zimbabwe
38764
Mr. F. Meyer

Westwood Wildlife Safaris
(Pvt.) Limited
P.O. Box 21
Victoria Falls
Zimbabwe
Victoria Falls 469
or 31519

Zimbabwe Game Association
Box 142
Ruwa Harare
Zimbabwe

Outfitters Directory: Hunting

Asia

Turkey

Pamfilya Hunting Org.
K-117
Antalya
Turkey
Mr. Y. Sobutay

Australia

Australia

Nimrod Safaris
P.O. Box 472
Darwin
Australia 5794
089-81-1633
089-81-1256
Mr. B. Lees

New Zealand

Angus Corporation Limited
P.O. Box 30069
Lower Hutt
New Zealand
NZ-04-663-329

Humboldt Hunting Safaris
P.O. Box 153
Queenstown
New Zealand
Mr. Gary Mullings

Lilybank Safari Lodge
P.O. Box 60
Lake Tekapo
New Zealand
064-5056-522
Mr. Gary Joll

New Zealand
Wildlife Safaris
P.O. Box 4058
Christchurch
New Zealand
Mr. Terry Pierson

Vern Wilson Hunting &
Shooting Consultants Ltd.
P.O. Box 7057
Hamilton
New Zealand
64-71-435-664

Westland Guiding Services
P.O. Box 38
Franz Josef Glacier
New Zealand
Ph 750 Telex Thru
4349
Mr. S. Peterson

Bimler, Harry
R.D. #2
Ngongotaha Rotorua
New Zealand
23457

Danks New Zealand Safaris
and Tours
P.O. Box 8066
Kensington Whangarei
New Zealand
Mr. A.C. Wilson

Europe

Austria

Worldwide Safaris
Krass 15
A-9560 Feldkirchen
Austria
04276-3692
Mr. Werner Fleck

Bulgaria

Bulgaria-Murgash
11 August-Str. 25
Sofia
Bulgaria 1000

England

Safari Services - International
P.O. Box 460
Windsor Berkshire
England SL44HN
07535-68341

Hunting Safari
Consultants of London
83 Gloucester Place
London W1H 3PG
England
01-486-4774
01-935-8996
Capt. J.C. Pollock

France

Safaris Jacques Guin
34, Route de Vinsobres
Valreas 84600
France
Mr. J. Guin

Holland

Worldwide Big Game
Safari Services
P.O. Box 40122
6504 AC Nijmegen
Holland
0-80-567778
31-80-584525
Mr. F. Duckworth

Outfitters Directory: Hunting

Europe

Hungary

State Farm
of Balatonnagybereki
Hun-Or Hunting Org.
Nimrod u. 1. Balatonfenyves
Hungary

Italy

Forum Travel
Thirama Grandi Cacce
00187 Roma
Via Veneto 23
Italy

Portugal

Urbanizacao Terplana
Lote 27 R/C D 2775
Parede
Portugal
246-4352
Mr. L.P. de Sa E Mello

Seia, Hugo Manuel
27685 Joao Do Estoril
Apartado 22 Estoril Codex
Portugal

Scotland

McCrave, Mike
Woodside
Gordon
Scotland TD36JU
057381-303

Sport in Scotland Ltd.
22 Market Brae
Inverness
Scotland 1V2 3AB
Mr. J. Ormiston

Spain

Cazaigerica
Mesones 5
Talavera de la Reina
Toledo
Spain
925-80-51-83
Mr. M.R. Benz

Cazatur
CIC Delegation
P.O. Box 50.577
Madrid 28080
Spain
Mr. Ricardo Medem

Spain Safaris
Box 752
Santiago
Spain
981-58-18-85
981-58-41-78
Dr. J. Varela-Duran

Trofeos International
c./Antonio Lopez 170,2
Madrid 28026
Spain
Mr. T. Garcia

Rosich Martin, Francisco
Professional Hunter
17 Cardenal Reig
2nd Floor, No. 1 Barcelona
Spain 08028
240-80-43
Mr. F. Rosich Martin

ACISA
Vereda de las Penas - La
Moraleja
Alcobendas Madrid
Spain
Mr. Bustamante

Huntinspain
P.O. Box 57
Majadahonda Madrid
Spain
Mr. A. Fabres

West Germany

Weinhold, Dieter
Auf Der Hohe 1
5204 Lohmar
West Germany
02246-4941

Wengert-Windrose Safari
Ltd.
Wiesensteigerstr .20
7341 Muehlausen
West Germany
011 37 7335-5204

North America

Canada: East

New Brunswick

Chickadee Lodge
Prince William NB
Canada EOH 1SO
506-363-2759 Lodge
506-363-2288
Mr. V. Schriver

Fundy Lodge
P.O. Box 1856
Woodstock NB
Canada EOJ 2BO
506-328-3571
506-755-2963

Gerald's Place
R.R. #1
Cody's, Queens Co. NB
Canada EOE 1EO
506-488-2737
Mr. G.C. Sarchfield

Hide Away Lodge
Box 820
Woodstock NB
Canada EOJ 2BO
506-894-2413
506-328-2272
Carrie and Ivan Hayden

Kelly's Sporting Lodge
Kelly Creek Basin
R.R. #6
Fredericton NB
Canada E3B 4X7
506-363-4435
Mr. Lorne MacDonald

Little Bald Peak Lodge
R.R. #1
Plaster Rock NB
Canada EOJ 1WO
506-356-2354
Mr. A. King

Outfitters Directory: Hunting

North America

Nepisiguit River Camps
R.R. #5, Box 345
Bathurst NB
Canada E2A 3Y8
506-546-5873
Mr. Kenneth Gray

The Old River Lodge
R.R. #2
Doaktown NB
Canada EOC 1GO
506-365-7568
Ms. Vicki Oland Mills

Webb, Fred A. and Sons
R.R. #1
Nictau, Plaster Rock NB
Canada EOJ 1WO
506-356-8312

Wild Country
Wilderness Outfitters
P.O. Box 148
Plaster Rock NB
Canada EOJ 1WO
506-356-2372
506-473-2907
Mr. J. Merritt

Newfoundland

MacInnis, Don
Highlands NFLD
Canada AON 1NO
709-639-7309

Pumphrey, Gerry
Highlands NFLD
Canada AON 1NO
709-645-2789

Reid, Mr. R.
P.O. Box 791
Corner Brook NFLD
Canada A2H 6G7
709-639-7258

Shanadithit Camps Ltd.
P.O. Box 733
Corner Brook NFLD
Canada A2H 6G7
709-634-2505
Mr. J. Peddle

Nova Scotia

Beaver Island Lodge
P.O. Box 402
Milton, Queen's County
N.S., Canada
BOT 1T0
902-354-4354

Clearwater Outfitters
R.R. #2
Annapolis NS
Canada BOS 1AO
902-638-3509
Robert and Marie

Lansdowne Lodge
Tom and Marion Kennedy
Upper Stewiacke Valley
NS Canada B0N 2P0
902-268-2749

Ontario

Canada North Outfitting Inc.
P.O. Box 1230 SA
Waterdown ONT
Canada L0R 2H0
416-689-7925

Northern Lights Resort
Box 79A
Loring ONT
Canada
705-757-2554
Mr. H. Stroeher

Polar Bear Camp
and Fly-In Outfitters
22-5th Street, P.O. Box 396
Cochrane ONT
Canada POL 1CO
705-272-5890
705-272-4672
Mr. S. Konopelky

Red Pine Hunting
and Fishing Camp
1402 Altona Road
Pickering ONT
Canada L1V 1M1
416-286-2994

Windy Bay Lodge
R.R. #1
Rainy River ONT
Canada POW 1LO
807-488-5723
416-298-6749
Mr. T. Beyak

Quebec

Arctic Adventures, c/o
8102 Trans Canada
Highway
Ville St. Laurent
Montreal QUE
Canada H4S 1R4
514-332-0880
Mr. S. Cantafio

Cerf-Sau Inc.
Dept. G
40 Racine Street
Loretteville QUE
Canada G2B 1C6
418-843-0173
Mr. Gilles Shooner

Domaine Omega Inc.
Route 323
Montebello QUE
Canada JOV 1LO
819-423-5023
Mr. Spengler

Laurentian Ungava
Outfitters Ltd.
R.R. #7
Lachute QUE
Canada J8H 3W9
514-562-3832
Mr. Jack Hume

Mistassini Lake
Outfitting Camps
Baie de Poste
Via Chibougamau QUE
Canada GOW 1CO
Mr. A. Matoosh

Montagnais Fishing and
Hunting Club
6357, Des Citelles
Orsainville QUE
Canada G1G 1E3
418-627-4165
418-585-2228
Mr. L. Valcourt

Nordik Adventure Inc.
P.O. Box 203 succ. LaSalle
LaSalle QUE
Canada H8R 3V2
514-366-7421

Normanic Inc.-Pourvoiries
Suite 103
2323, Boul. du Versant Nord
Sainte-Foy QUE
Canada G1N 4P4
418-681-1258
Mr. F. Lacombe

Pourvoirie des
100 Lacs, Inc.
603, Boul. Ste-Elisabeth (#A)
La Prairie QUE
Canada J5R 1V5
514-659-4155

Outfitters Directory: Hunting

North America

Pourvoyeurs de
la Riviere Delay Inc.
C.P. 1540
Schefferville QUE
Canada GOG 2TO
418-585-3475 Wint
418-585-3775 Summ

Richer Lodge (Echouani)
c/o Raymond Richer
110 Cavanaugh
Maniwaki QUE
Canada J9E 2P8
819-449-1613
AlmaRadio 514-181

Toundratour Inc.
Chambeaux Club
319 East, St. Zotique
Montreal QUE
Canada H2S 1L5
514-270-7266
Mr. Henri Poupart

Tuktu Fishing & Hunting Club
Box 427
Ancienne-Lorette QUE
Canada G2E 4W6
418-872-3839

Hunt River Camps Ltd.
P.O. Box 307, Station A
Goose Bay, Labrador NFLD
Canada AOP 1SO

Canada North

Northwest Territories

Arctic Fishing Lodges
& Outfitters
Box 806
Yellowknife NWT
Canada X1A 2N6
403-873-4036
403-873-3626
Ms. Yvonne Quick

Guided Arctic Expeditions
P.O. Box 2120
Inuvik NWT
Canada X0E 0T0
403-979-2408
Mr. T. Cook

Guided Arctic Expeditions
Box 2000
Inuvik NWT
Canada XOE OTO
403-979-3510
Mr. J. Amos

Mackenzie Mountain
Outfitters Ltd.
Box 124
Norman Wells NWT
Canada XOE OVO
403-587-2255
Mr. S. Stevens

Webb-Qaivvik Ltd.
441 Church Rd.
Landsdale Pa. 19446
215-362-1510

True North Safaris
36 Morrison Drive
Yellowknife NWT
Canada X1A 1Z2
403-873-8533
Mr. G. Jaeb

Yukon Territory

Belle Desrosiers
Box 4804
Whitehorse Yukon
Canada Y1A 4N6
403-633-2146

Cassiar Mountain
Outfitters (1979) Ltd.
P.O. Box 267
Watson Lake Yukon
Canada YOA 1CO
403-536-7536
Mr. K. Funnell

Ceaser Lake Outfitters
Box 484
Watson Lake Yukon
Canada YOA 1CO
403-536-2174
Mr. T. Wilkinson

Dickson, R.A. (Dick)
708 Minto Rd.
Whitehorse Yukon
Canada Y1A 3X9
403-633-2228

Dolhan, Ed
High Country Safaris Ltd.
Teslin Yukon
Canada YOA 1BO
Radio, JJ 36454
Swift River

Hidden Valley Outfitters Ltd.
General Delivery
Carmacks Yukon
Canada YOB 1CO
Radio Phone
2M 2572 Carmacks
Ms. D. Marino

Jennings River Outfitters
P.O. Box 5299
Whitehorse Yukon
Canada Y1A 4Z2
Whitehorse Mobile
Op.White Mountain
Mr. Jon Jennings

Jensen, Pete
58 Alsek Rd.
Whitehorse Yukon
Canada Y1A 3K4
403-667-2030

Koser, Mr. Werner
General Delivery
Ross River Yukon
Canada YOB 1SO
403-969-2210

Kusawa Outfitters Ltd.
28 Alsek Road
Whitehorse Yukon
Canada
403-667-2755
403-667-2379
Mr. K. Heynen

Low, Doug J.
General Delivery
Tagish Yukon
Canada YOB 1TO
403-821-4515

MacMillan River
Outfitters, Inc.
Box 5088
Whitehorse Yukon
Canada Y1A 4S3
403-668-5072
Mr. D. Coleman

Ostashek Outfitting Ltd.
Box 4146
Whitehorse Yukon
Canada Y1A 3S6
403-668-7323
Mr. J.L. Ostashek

Reynolds, Stan
Box 108
Dawson City Yukon
Canada YOB 1GO
H.F. Radio SQ 787

Outfitters Directory: Hunting

North America

Rogue River Outfitters
General Delivery
Ross River Yukon
Canada YOB 1SO
403-969-2250

Ruby Range Outfitters
General Delivery
Destruction Bay Yukon
Canada YOA 1HO
Mr. J. Drift

Young, David
Site 12, Comp. 24, R.R. #1
Whitehorse Yukon
Canada Y1A 4Z6
403-668-4518

Yukon Hunting &
Guiding Ltd.
#25 - 5 Klondike Rd.
Whitehorse Yukon
Canada Y1A 3L7
403-667-7182
Mr. R. Hardie

Yukon Outfitting
Box 5364-T
Whitehorse Yukon
Canada Y1A 4Z2
403-667-2712
Mr. R. Furniss

Canada West

Alberta

Alberta Rocky Mountain
Outfitters
R.R. #1
Bon Accord AL
Canada TOA OKO
Mr. L. Ferbey

Alberta Trophy Hunters
#265 Scot Haven
52246 Rge. Road 232
Sherwood Park AL
Canada T8B 1C1
403-467-9598
403-467-8668

Alberta Trophy Hunts
Box 1563
Hinton AL
Canada TOE 1BO
403-865-3990
Mr. Ferlin Koma

Americana Expeditions Inc.,
Hunting Consultants
4707-106A, Suite 19
Edmonton AL
Canada T6A 1J3
403-469-0579
403-468-1060
Mr. P. Frederick

Arctic Red River
Outfitters Ltd.
Box 1457
Lloydminster AL
Canada S9V 1K4
403-875-0560
403-875-8926
Mr. R. Woodward

Artindale Guide Service
Box 2642
Olds AL
Canada TOM 1PO
403-335-8532
Mr. Doug Artindale

Ayers, Don
3015 109th Avenue
Edmonton AL
Canada T5W OG2
403-433-5395 days
403-479-4433 eve.

Barrier Mountain Outfitters
Box 69
Olds AL
Canada TOM 1PO
403-556-6778
Mr. W. Les Short

Double Diamond
Wilderness Trails
R.R. #3
Rimbey AL
Canada TOC 2JO
403-843-3582
Mr. John Hatala

Hartnum, Bruce
2411 - 49 St.
Edmonton AL
Canada T6L 4P4
403-450-HUNT
403-463-9470

Jake's Guide & Outfitting
Box 684
Sundre AL
Canada TOM 1XO
403-638-4071
Mr. D. Vennard

K Country Outfitting
Box 1343
Cochrane AL
Canada TOL OWO
403-932-6088
Mr. K. Koebisch

Kostynuk, Sam
Outfitting
P.O. Box 636
Rocky Mt. House AL
Canada TOM 1TO
403-845-2197
403-845-6620

Leonard Outfitting Ltd.
Box 818
Grande Cache AL
Canada TOE OYO
403-827-3246

McKenzie's M7
Trails West
Box 971
Rocky Mountain House AL
Canada TOM 1TO
403-845-6708
Mr. E. McKenzie

Nahanni Butte Outfitters Ltd.
Box 879
Nanton AL
Canada TOL 1RO
403-646-5768
Mr. G. Williams

NWT Outfitters Ltd.
Box 1144
Glenwood AL
Canada TOK 2RO
403-626-3279
Mr. D. Nelson

Pacific Rim Guide Service
#7-2016 Sherwood Dr.
Sherwood Park AL
Canada T8A 3X3
Mr. R. D. Munroe

Porcupine Creek Outfitters
Box 2442
Pincher Creek AL
Canada TOK 1WO
403-627-2540
Mr. B. Sinclair

Ram Head Outfitters Ltd.
Box 1517
Claresholm AL
Canada TOL OTO
403-652-2931
403-625-2207

Outfitters Directory: Hunting

North America

Ramhead Outfitters Inc.
Box 89
Warburg AL
Canada TOC 2TO
403-848-7578
403-848-2502
Mr. S. Simpson

Redstone Mountain Trophy
Hunts
Box 608
Banff AL
Canada TOL OCO
403-762-5241
403-388-2117
Tim and Hugh MacAulay

Rifle Creek Guiding Service
10827-38A Avenue
Edmonton AL
Canada T6J OL6
Mr. D. Till

Rocky Mountain Safaris Inc.
Unit 13, 2020 105 Street
Edmonton AL
Canada T6J5J2
403-437-3101

South Nahanni Outfitters Ltd.
Box 586
Cardston AL
Canada TOK OKO
403-653-2562
Mr. B. Woodward

Steve Cooper Outfitters
P.O. Box 1347
Edmonton AL
Canada T5J 2N2
403-477-6595

Stricker's Outfitting Ltd
Box 354
Wildwood AL
Canada TOE 2MO
403-325-3961

Timbermountain Packtrain
Box 511
Claresholm AL
Canada TOL OTO
403-625-2931
Mr. D.D. Simpson

Trangen, Eric
Guide/Outfitter
Box 174
Bashaw AL
Canada TOB OHO

Trimble Outfitting
P.O. Box 209
Caroline AL
Canada TOM OMO
403-722-2340
Ms. Janet Trimble

Trophy Hunting & Fishing
Consultants Ltd.
12 Cedardale Cr. S.W.
Calgary AL
Canada T2W 3Z5
403-251-3828
Mr. L.D. Biscope

Turner, R.W. (Bobby)
R.R. #2
Cochrane AL
Canada TOL OWO
403-932-5504

Vinson, Tom
Bonded Outfitter
and Class 'A' Guide
Brule AL
Canada TOE OCO
403-865-4777

Wiens Whitetails Inc.
Site 1, Box 6, R.R. #2
Tofield AL
Canada TOB 4JO
403-662-3963
Mr. E. Wiens

British Columbia

A/Z Ranch Ltd.
Box 86
Windermere BC
Canada VOB 2LO
Mr. Bill Dubois

Alpine Mountain Outfitters
Box 821
Chetwynd BC
Canada VOC 1JO
Fixed Base
Radio Telephone

Ashnola Guide-Outfitters
Box 122
Keremeos BC
Canada VOX 1NO
604-499-5853
Mr. C. Schneider

Aurora Outfitters
Box 4150
Smithers BC
Canada VOJ 2NO
604-847-4848
Mr. K. Oysmueller

Bear Paw Guides and
Outfitters
General Delivery
Sinclair Mills BC
Canada VOJ 3MO
Mr. D. Smith

Big Game Guide and
Outfitters
General Delivery
Dome Creek BC
Canada VOJ 1HO
Mr. K. W. Hooker

Bougie Mountain Outfitters
R.R. #1, Mile 308, Box 30
Ft. Nelson BC
Canada VOC 1RO
Mr. P. Gillis

Caribou Mountain Outfitters
P.O. Box 4010
Quesnel BC
Canada V2J 3J2
604-747-3334
Mr. B. Bowden

Carson, John and Rita
P.O. Box 1977
Grand Forks BC
Canada VOH 1HO
604-442-2406

Diamond M Outfitters Ltd.
P.O. Box 297
Atlin BC
Canada VOW 1AO
Radio Phone 2M8464
White Mtn. Channel
Mr. Jim Mattarozzo

Doern, Wally
566 Edkins Street
Quesnel BC
Canada V2J 1X9
604-992-2287

Double Eagle Guides
and Outfitters
Box 11, SS #1
Granisle BC
Canada VOJ 1WO
Mr. S. Berg

Driftwood Ventures
SS #3, Comp. 1, Sykes Rd.
Prince George BC
Canada V2N 2S7
604-964-2467
Mr. S.S. Schielke

Outfitters Directory: Hunting

North America

East Kootenay Outfitters
14-21st Avenue S.
Cranbrook BC
Canada V1C 3H1
604-426-2834
Mr. J. Juozaitis

Elk Valley Bighorn
Outfitters Ltd.
Box 414
Fernie BC
Canada VOB 1MO
604-529-7209
Mr. B. Fontana

Fawnie Mountain Outfitters
General Delivery
Anahim Lake BC
Canada VOL 1CO
Pr.George Radio Ph
H487487 Nimpo Chnl
Mr. John Blackwell

Finlay River Outfitters
549 Lampson St.
Victoria BC
Canada V9A 5Z8
604-385-3649

Frontier Hunting
Box 4491
Quesnel BC
Canada V2J 3J4
Mr. D. Davis

Gana River Outfitters Ltd.
Box 1178, Station A
Kelowna BC
Canada V1Y 7P8
604-763-0685
Mr. G. Koopman

Gana River Outfitters
Box 4659
Quesnel BC
Canada V2J 3J8
604-992-8639
Mr. B. McKenzie

Glenora Guest Ranch Ltd.
Telegraph Creek BC
Canada VOJ 2WO
Radiophone
JJ3-7079 Meehause
Mrs. B. Nancy Ball

Graham River
Outfitters, Ltd.
Fort St. John BC
Canada V1J 4H9
604-785-4250
Radio YJ3-6280
Ms. Audrey Tompkins

Indian River Ranch
P.O. Box 360
Atlin BC
Canada VOW 1AO
Mr. D. Smith

Kettle River Guides
R.R. #1
Oliver BC
Canada OOH 1TO
Mr. M. Kilback

Kimsquit
Fishing Outfitters
R.R. #4, Site 17, Comp. 17
Prince George BC
Canada V2N 2J2
Mr. G. Pittman

Lamoureux Outfitters Ltd.
General Delivery
Ft. Ware BC
Canada VOJ 3BO
Ft.Nelson Radio Op
2M3827 Ft. Ware
Mr. M. Lamoureux

Len's Guide Service
Box 825
Prince George BC
Canada V2L 4T7
N698736 Radio Op.
Mr. L. Pickering

Monashee Guide Service
R.R. #1
Lumby BC
Canada VOW 1AO
Mr. J. Langton

Moon Lake Outfitters Ltd.
P.O. Box 161
Atlin BC
Canada VOW 1AO
604-651-7515
Mr. E. Smith

Purcell Wilderness
Guiding & Outfitting
Box 6, Site 15, S.S. #1
Kimberley BC
Canada V1A 2Y3
604-427-7295
Mr. G. Hansen

Ram Creek Outfitters
General Delivery
Wardner BC
Canada VOB 2JO
604-429-3445
Mr. R. Fahselt

Red Sorensen Outfitting
Dept. SG, Box 6067
Victoria BC
Canada V8P 5L4
604-785-6473
N417452 Muncho Lk.

Rocky Mountain High
Outfitter & Guides
P.O. Box 65
Wardner BC
Canada VOB 2JO
604-429-3560
Mr. B. Scott

Ruby Range Outfitters Ltd.
Box 4874
Williams Lake BC
Canada V2G 2V8
604-398-7686
604-296-4305
Mr. John Drift

Sheep Mountain Outfitters
Box 577
Fernie BC
Canada VOB 1MO
604-423-7136

Simons, Charlie
Guide/Outfitter
P.O. Box 141
Horsefly BC
Canada VOL 1LO

Skeena Mountain Outfitters
6821 Lilac Crescent
Prince George BC
Canada V2K 3H2
604-962-7995
Mr. V. Carson

Sorensen, R.
Guide/Outfitter
Box 40
Muncho Lake BC
Canada VOC 1ZO

Spatsizi
Collingwood Bros. Guides
P.O. Box 3070
Smithers BC
Canada VOJ 2NO
604-847-9692 Days
604-846-9196

Steciw, I.
Box 2665
Smithers BC
Canada VOJ 2NO
604-847-3055

Outfitters Directory: Hunting

North America

Stein River Outfitters Ltd.
P.O. Box 494
Hope BC
Canada V0X 1LO
604-869-9532
Mr. Leo Ouellet

Stone Mountain Safaris
Mile 422, Alaska Highway
Toad River BC
Canada V1G 4J8
604-232-5469
Mr. D. Wiens

Taku Safari Inc.
P.O. Box 268
Atlin BC
Canada V0W 1AO
Mr. G. Anttila

Taseko Lake Outfitters
Box 4834
Williams Lake BC
Canada V2G 2V8
N424967 Mob.Op.
Prince George BC
Mr. S. Henry

Tweedsmuir Park Guides
Box 569
Vanderhoof BC
Canada V0J 3AO
Mr. B. Nielsen

Manitoba

Mantagao Outfitters Inc.
15 Wiltshire Bay
Winnipeg MAN
Canada R2J 2L6
204-235-0557

Saskatchewan

Sportsmen's Adventures Inc.
94 Empress Drive
Regina SASK
Canada S4T 6M6
306-522-6381

United States
North East

Connecticut

M'Dalla Safari Company
Oak Point Club
New Milford CT
USA 06776
203-355-1945
Mr. T.M. Sweeney

Iowa

Hitzhusen Hunts
and Sporting Goods
304 Main Street,
P.O. Box 420
Rockwell IA
USA 50469
515-822-4688
515-822-3300
Mr. D. Hitzhusen

Keeline, Jim H.
Registered Guide
Box 7044
Spirit Lake IA
USA 51360
712-336-5124
712-225-2168

Illinois

Adventure Safaris Ltd.
Ste. #747, Three First Ntl.
Plaza
Chicago IL
USA 60602
312-782-4756
Mr. P. Merzig

ISI Worldwide Adventures,
Ltd.
P.O. Drawer 440
Carpentersville IL
USA 60110
312-428-3311
Mr. George Daniels

Massachusetts

Boston Safaris Ltd.
Shrewsbury Street
West Boylston MA
USA 01583
617-835-6057

Maine

Foggy Mountain Guide
Service
R.F.D. 2, Box 103
Dover-Foxcroft ME
USA 04426
207-564-3404
Mr. W.A. Bosowicz

Gentle Ben's Hunting &
Fishing Lodge
Box 212, SI
Rockwood ME
USA 04478
207-534-2201
Mr. B. Pelletier

Hooke's Guide Service
P.O. Box 257, Route 4
Strong ME
USA 04983
207-684-4178
Mr. T. Hooke

Mountain View Lodge
H.C.R. 76, Box 20
Greenville ME
USA 04441
207-695-3882
Mr. D. Peters

Patten Hunting Lodge
C/O 38 Preble Street
Portland ME
USA 04101
207-772-0548 Bus.
207-657-3867 Res.
Mr. B. Finney

Reid, Raymond
Box 820
Thorndike ME
USA 04986
207-568-3165
709-639-7258

Michigan

International Big Game
Safaris
100 S. Waverly Road
Holland MI
USA 49423
616-392-6458

Renegade Ranch
2690 Riggsville Road
Cheboygan MI
USA 49721
616-627-9744
Mr. W. Romanik

Safari Adventures Ltd.
1929 Lone Pine Road
Bloomfield Hills MI
USA 48013
313-851-1707
Mr. C. Bazzy

New Hampshire

Wilderness Adventures
17 Woodlawn Ridge
Concord NH
USA 03301
603-224-7578

Outfitters Directory: Hunting

North America

New Jersey

Landela Safaris, C/O
Ventures International
Weldon Rd., R.D. 3
Lake Hopatcong NJ
USA 07849
Mr. K. Boehme

Orion Trophy Expeditions
Outfitters
R.D. E3, Box 472
Phillipsburg NJ
USA 08865
201-859-1584

New York

Global Outdoors
85 Johanna Lane
Staten Island NY
USA 10309
718-317-7895
Mr. A. Cito

Rieder, Rory
44 Kane Avenue
Larchmont NY
USA 10538
914-834-5611

Wilderness Trek
4417 Grandview Avenue
Hamburg NY
USA 14075
Mr. P. McDonnell

Wildtrak Inc.
Box 500S
Honeoye NY
USA 14471
716-229-2700

Ohio

Basset, D. Lee
30201 Aurora Road
Cleveland OH
USA 44139

Grants Cabins
191 E. Washington Avenue
Marion OH
USA 43302
614-387-5571

Whitetail Outfitters
75117 Johnson Run Road
Guernsey OH
USA 43749
614-498-6443 Ohio
616-937-4351 Mich
Mr. A. Prisbe

Pennsylvania

Foulkrod's Archery Camp
R.D. 1, Box 140
Troy PA
USA 16947
717-297-4367
717-297-3806
Mr. B. Foulkrod

Hemlock Acres
R.D. #3 SC
Benton PA
USA 17814
717-458-5143

Jim McCarthy Adventures
4906 Creek Drive
Harrisburg PA
USA 17112
717-652-4374
717-545-1952

Martz's Game Farm
R.D. 1, Box 85
Dalmatia PA
USA 17017
717-758-3307 Har
717-758-1535 Don
Harold or Don Martz

Outfitters Unlimited Inc.
P.O. Box 11940, Federal
Square Stn.
Harrisburg PA
USA 17108
717-766-0789
Mr. B. Dunn

Safaris Africa
3995 School Road South
Jeannette PA
USA 15644
412-733-2878

Tioga Boar Hunting Preserve
Road Number 1
Tioga PA
USA 16946
717-835-5341

Webb Quaivvik Ltd.
441 Church Road
Lansdale PA
USA 19446·
215-362-1510

World Hunts Inc.
P.O. Box 777
Latrobe PA
USA 15650
412-537-7668
1-800-4-HUNTING

Wisconsin

Hunts West
139 Hwy 10 West
Stevens Point WI
USA 54481
715-344-HUNT

United States North West

Alaska

AAA Alaskan Outfitters
P.O. Box 110-774
Anchorage AK
USA 99511-0774
907-345-0399

AAA Alaskan Outfitters
2820 Lexington Ave.
Anchorage AK
USA 99502
907-243-1067
Mr. R.D. Morris

Alaska Hunting Consultants
12720 Saunders Road
Anchorage AK
USA 99516
907-345-1535
Mr. R. Reed

Alaska Hunts
2900 Boniface Parkway #607
Anchorage AK
USA 99504
907-333-5214
Mr. C. Engle

Alaska Trophy Hunts
Mystic Lake Lodge
Box 878
Palmer AK
USA 99645
907-745-3168
George or Marty Palmer

Alaskan Trophy Hunting
Box 193-A-1
Willow AK
USA 99688
907-495-6434
Mr. Dick Gunlogson

Arctic Alaska Safaris
P.O. Box 57
Kotzebue AK
USA 99752
907-442-3592
Mr. John A. Walker

Outfitters Directory: Hunting

North America

Bailey, James K.
P.O. Box 770695
Eagle River AK
USA 99577
907-688-2163

Black, Stephen W.
P.O. Box 4323
Kenai AK
USA 99611

Branham, Chris
P.O. Box 6184
Anchorage AK
USA 99502

Branham, Mike
P.O. Box 190128
Anchorage AK
USA 99519-0128

Brooks Range Arctic Hunts
Parks Hwy., Mile 329, Rt. 1
Nenana AK
USA 99760
Mr. E. Witt

Canoe Bay Outfitters
P.O. Box 176
Sand Point AK
USA 99661
907-383-2381
907-383-3844
Mr. S. Hakala, Sr.

Carlson, Dick
3900 Greenland Dr.
Anchorage AK
USA 99517

Castle, Lynn
Master Guide
P.O. Box 517
Denali Park AK
USA 99755

Cinder River Lodge
1820 Rebel Ridge Dr.
Anchorage AK
USA 99504
Mr. G. King Jr.

Deneut, Michael C.
Pope & Vannoy Landing
Iliamna AK
USA 99606

Driver, Philip E.
1306 E. 26th Avenue
Anchorage AK
USA 99508

Engle, Clark L.
2900 Boniface, #607
Anchorage AK
USA 99504

Englund, Des
P.O. Box 6881
Anchorage AK
USA 99502

Erickson, John E.
P.O. Box 101
Tok AK
USA 99780

Exclusive Alaskan Hunts
Rt. C, Box 8860
Palmer AK
USA 99645
Mr. A. Runyan

Fair Chase Hunts
P.O. Box 10-2104
Anchorage AK
USA 99510-2104
907-274-3996
Mr. J. Hendricks

Fait, Gary
1013 E. Diamond Blvd., #507
Anchorage AK
USA 99502
907-345-1731

Fanning, Ken
P.O. Box 80929
College AK
USA 99708

Farmen, Darrell
1200 E. 76th Avenue, Ste.
1228
Anchorage AK
USA 99518

Fejes, Samuel T.
P.O. Box 111394
Anchorage AK
USA 99511

Fitzgerald, Bill
P.O. Box 93
Talkeetna AK
USA 99676

Fitzgerald, Kevin
P.O. Box 375
Talkeetna AK
USA 99676

Flynn, David H.
9800 Tolsona Circle
Anchorge AK
USA 99502

Flynn, Howard D.
4203 Minnesota Drive
Anchorage AK
USA 99503

Frazier, Jay
P.O. Box 1331
Delta Junction AK
USA 99737

Frost, Stan
P.O. Box 112449
Anchorage AK
USA 99511

Gaedeke, Bernd
P.O. Box 80424
Farmers Loop Road
Fairbanks AK
USA 99708

Gay, Kirk D.
P.O. Box 6583
Anchorage AK
USA 99502

Gerlach, Robert
P.O. Box 23
Talkeetna AK
USA 99676

Gillis, Melvin B.
847 E. 74th
Anchorage AK
USA 99502

Glacier Guides Inc.
P.O. Box 66
Gustavus AK
USA 99826
907-697-2252
Mr. J. Rosenbruch

Grasser, Ed
P.O. Box 1350
Palmer AK
USA 99645

Gray, Charles Lee
311 Slater Street
Fairbanks AK
USA 99701

Guthrie, Richard A.
P.O. Box 24-0163
9530 Albatross Drive
Anchorage AK
USA 99524
907-243-7766

Hancock, Lee
Nabesna Road
Slana AK
USA 99586

Outfitters Directory: Hunting

North America

Hankerd, Hank
P.O. Box 873668
Wasilla AK
USA 99687

Hannon, Bob
General Delivery, Box 22
Koyuk AK
USA 99753
907-963-3221

Hansen, David
1511 Atkinson
Anchorage AK
USA 99504

Harms, Dennis
P.O. Box 670071
Chugiak AK
USA 99567

Harrower, Jim
13830 Jarvis Drive
Anchorage AK
USA 99515

Hautanen, Nelson
3157 64th Avenue
Anchorage AK
USA 99502

Helmericks, Harmon
930 9th Avenue
Fairbanks AK
USA 99701

Herscher, Rick
Box 8376
Anchorage AK
USA 99508
907-279-9874

High Adventure
Air Charter, Guides/Outf.
P.O. Box 486
Soldotna AK
USA 99669
907-262-5237
Mr. W. Bell

Holleman, Dan Foy
P.O. Box 80085
Fairbanks AK
USA 99708

Hunt Alaska
Chisana AK
USA 99588
Mr. T. Overly

Ingledue, F.W.
4815 Glacier Highway
Juneau AK
USA 99801

Israelson, Arnold J.
Box 467
Yakutat AK
USA 99689

J & P Enterprises
2999 Dyke Road
North Pole AK
USA 99705
907-488-1534

Jacobson, J.P. 'Jake'
P.O. Box 124
Kotzebue AK
USA 99752

Jacobson, Patricia A.
P.O. Box 1313
Kodiak AK
USA 99615

Jensen, Marcus F.
P.O. Box 2220
Juneau AK
USA 99802

Johnson, Don L.
P.O. Box 152
Kenai AK
USA 99611

Johnson, Keith
3646 N. Point Drive
Anchorage AK
USA 99502
907-243-5087

Johnson, Warren
Bear Lake Lodge
Port Moller AK
USA 99571

Jones' Guide & Outfitting
HCR 33675 Jones Drive
Homer AK
USA 99603
907-235-6455

Kahn, Steve
SR Box 26192
Wasilla AK
USA 99687

Katmai Guide Service
Box 313
King Salmon AK
USA 99613
907-246-3030
Mr. Joe Klutsch

Keeline, Jim
P.O. Box 1333
Juneau AK
USA 99801
712-336-5124
712-225-2168

Keen, Rocky
SRA Box 6316
Palmer AK
USA 99654

King Jr., Gary
1820 Rebel Ridge Drive
Anchorage AK
USA 99504

Knutson, Howard
Suite 211
555 W. Northern Lights Blvd.
Anchorage AK
USA 99503

Kusko Kwim Guide Service
1608 Tamarack St., #2
Fairbanks AK
USA 99701
Mr. P. Shepherd

Lamoureux, Gus & Frenchy
P.O. Box 4-444-S
Anchorage AK
USA 99509
907-248-4971
907-248-3012

Lane, Karl E.
P.O. Box 295
Juneau AK
USA 99802

LaRose, Gary B.
P.O. Box 3412
Palmer AK
USA 99645

Latham, John H.
P.O. Box 254
Yakutat AK
USA 99689

Lazer, David L.
Master Guide
SRA Box 6877
Palmer AK
USA 99645
907-745-4504

Lee, Jack
P.O. Box 4-2495
Anchorage AK
USA 99509

Outfitters Directory: Hunting

North America

Lee, Tony
P.O. Box 771224-S AP
Eagle River AK
USA 99577

Leonard, Dave
P.O. Box 1426
Kenai AK
USA 99611

Lovin, Lloyd K.
P.O. Box 81429
College AK
USA 99708

Matfay, Larry
P.O. Box 2
Old Harbor AK
USA 99643

McNutt, Ray
Box 10
Sterling AK
USA 99672

Metheny, Jim
P.O. Box 40015
Clear AK
USA 99704

Midnight Sun Adventures
1306 E. 26th Ave.
Anchorage AK
USA 99508
Mr. P. Driver

Morgan, Rocky
P.O. Box 870649
Wasilla AK
USA 99687

Mountain Monarchs
of Alaska
P.O. Box 1426
Kenai AK
USA 99611
907-283-4010
907-694-1569
Mr. D. Leonard

Neel, Dave
P.O. Box 6303
Anchorage AK
USA 99502

Norman, Edward M.
P.O. Box 770588
Eagle River AK
USA 99577

Nunivak Outfitters
Box 2
Mekoryuk AK
USA 99630
Mr. F. Don

Oney, Tony
2631 W. 100th Avenue
Anchorage AK
USA 99515

Overly, Terry
Pioneer Outfitters
Chisana AK
USA

Owens, Dennis C.
P.O. Box 61
Moose Pass AK
USA 99631

Pahl, Gerald
P.O. Box 516
Glennallen AK
USA 99588

Park Munsey, Michael
Amook Pass
Kodiak AK
USA 99615

Peninsula Outfitters and
Air Taxi
P.O. Box 1444
Kenai AK
USA 99611
907-776-5578

Pinnell, Bill
Olga Bay
Kodiak AK
USA 99615

Ptarmigan Lake Lodge
1001 Lake View Terrace
Fairbanks AK
USA 99701
907-456-6967
Mr. Urban E. Rahoi

Quest Charters
510 W. Tudor, Ste. #5
Anchorage AK
USA 99503
907-562-2628
Mr. Michael Norman

Rainbow River Lodge
Northwest Outfitters
4127 Rasberry Road
Anchorage AK
USA 99502
Mr. Chris Goll

Reiner, Dennis E.
P.O. Box 55454
North Pole AK
USA 99705

Rivers, Larry R.
P.O. Box 107
Talkeetna AK
USA 99676
907-733-2471

Rohrer's Bear Camp
Box 2219
Kodiak AK
USA 99615
907-486-5835
Mr. Richard Rohrer

Running W Outfitters
Star Route A, Box 49-H
Homer AK
USA 99603
Mr. D. Wade

Runyan, Andy
SRC Box 8860
Palmer AK
USA 99645

Sage, C. Michael
5108 Strawberry Road
Anchorage AK
USA 99502

Schetzle, Harold
P.O. Box 670790
Chugiak AK
USA 99567

Schoonover, Ken
Box 136
Hoonah AK
USA 99829

Shavings, Ed
P.O. Box 31
Mekoryuk AK
USA 99630

Sheep River Hunting Camps
C/O P.O. Box 87-1721 or
P.O. Box 87-5149
Wasilla AK
USA 99687
Mr. E. Stevenson

Shepherd, Pete
1721 University Ave., C-25
Fairbanks AK
USA 99701

Outfitters Directory: Hunting

North America

Smith, Tarleton F.
Box 1132
Sitka AK
USA 99835

Spiridon Camp
Box 483
Kodiak AK
USA 99615
907-486-5436
Mr. L. Francisco

Stoney River Lodge
P.O. Box 670577
Chugiak AK
USA 99567
907-688-2187
Mr. C. Warren

Swiss's
Alaska Trophy Hunts
129 F Street
Anchorage AK
USA 99501
907-272-1725
Mr. John Swiss

Talaheim Lodge
4505 Spenard Road, #205
Anchorage AK
USA 99517
907-733-2815
Mr. Mark Miller

Talifson, Morris
Olga Bay
Kodiak AK
USA 99615

Timberline Outfitters
Box 134, Dept. 49T
Chugiak AK
USA 99567
907-688-2722
Mr. E.E. 'Red' Beeman

Tinker, Mike
Box 197
Ester AK
USA 99725

Troutman, Donald
2453 Homestead Drive
North Pole AK
USA 99705

Van Veenen, Erik
Reg. Guide
General Delivery
Ester AK
USA 99725

Vince, Gary
Muskwa Safaris
Fort St. John AK
USA

Vrem, Kelly
P.O. Box 670742
Chugiak AK
USA 99567
907-688-3736

Vrem, Tracy
P.O. Box 520623
Big Lake AK
USA 99652

Warren, Curly
P.O. Box 670577
Chugiak AK
USA 99567

Waugaman, William
P.O. Box 80589
College AK
USA 99708

Webber, Mike
P.O. Box 670748
Chugiak AK
USA 99567

Wetzel, Dan L.
P.O. Box 10224
22 Mile Cks. Road
Fairbanks AK
USA 99710

White, Ben
1513 F Street
Anchorage AK
USA 99501

Wildman Lake Lodge
3646 N. Point Dr.
Anchorage AK
USA
Mr. K. Johnson

Wirschem, Charles
6608 Blackberry Street
Anchorage AK
USA 99502

Worker, Matt
P.O. Box 871574
Wasilla AK
USA 99687

Idaho

Anderson Outfitting
4990 Valenty Road, Dept. P
Pocatello ID
USA 83202
208-237-6544 Day
208-237-2664 Night
Mr. Rbt. B. Anderson

Barker River Trips
2124 Grelle
Lewiston ID
USA 83501
208-743-7459
Mr. J. Barker

Beamer's Heller Bar
Box 1223
Lewiston ID
USA 83501
208-743-4800
Ms. M. Beamer

Bear River Outfitters
Star Route 1, Box 1450
Montpelier ID
USA 83254
208-847-0263
Mr. M. Jensen

Bighorn Outfitters
Box 66
Carmen ID
USA 83462
208-756-3407
Mr. M. McFarland

Boulder Creek Outfitters
Incorporated
Box 119
Peck ID
USA 83545
208-486-6232
208-839-2282
Mr. T. Craig

Butler, Bruce
Box 478
Hailey ID
USA 83333
208-788-2468

Castle Creek Outfitters
Box 2008
Salmon ID
USA 83467
208-344-6600
Mr. D. McAfee

Outfitters Directory: Hunting

North America

Cat Track Outfitters
113 East Avenue C
Jerome ID
USA 83338
208-324-3337
Mr. T. Molitor

Chamberlain Basin Outfitters
Route 1, Box 240-A
Salmon ID
USA 83467
208-756-3715

Chilly Ranch
Star Route
Mackay ID
USA 83251
208-588-2584
Mr. M. Butler

Clearwater Outfitters
4088 Canyon Creek Road
Orofino ID
USA 83544
208-476-5971
Mr. L. Crane

Coolwater Outfitters
HC 75, Box 63
Kooskia ID
USA 83539
208-926-4707
Mr. Don Wilson

Cross Outfitters
310 South 3rd East
Preston ID
USA 83263
208-852-1038
Mr. L.W. Cross

Custom River Tours
Box 7071
Boise ID
USA 83707
208-343-3343
Mr. K. Masoner

Diamond D Ranch Inc.
Box 1
Clayton ID
USA 83227
313-773-5850
Mr. T. Demorest

Dixie Outfitters Inc.
Box 33
Dixie ID
USA 83525
208-842-2417
Mr. W.E. Smith

Eakin Ridge Outfitters Inc.
Box 1382
Salmon ID
USA 83467
208-756-2047
Mr. Lamont Anderson

Elk River Outfitters
Box 265
Orofino ID
USA 83544
208-476-7074
Mr. Mike Stockton

Epley's Idaho Outdoor
Adventure
Box 987
McCall ID
USA 83638
208-634-5173

F M & R Outfitters
HCR-01, Box 300
Naples ID
USA 83847
208-267-5993
208-267-8903
Mr. Jack Riddle

Flying Resort Ranches Inc.
Box 770
Salmon ID
USA 83467
208-756-6295
Mr. William R. Guth

Garden Valley Outfitters Inc.
Garden Valley ID
USA 83622
208-462-3751
Mr. Dan Rotthoff

Gillihan's Guide Service
850 Jackson Ave.
Emmett ID
USA 83617
208-365-2750
Mr. Bob Gillihan

Gilmore Ranch Outfitters
and Guides
Box 641
Grangeville ID
USA 83530
208-983-2196
Mr. Chuck Neill

Happy Hollow Camps
Star Route, Box 14
Salmon ID
USA 83467
208-756-3954
Mr. Martin Capps

Harrah's Middle Fork Lodge
3815 Rickenbacker
Boise ID
USA 83705
208-342-7888
208-342-7941
Mr. Nick Stuparich

Idaho Big Game, Inc.
P.O. Box 2501
Salmon ID
USA 83467
208-756-4407
Mr. Jon Goodman

Idaho Guide Service Inc.
Box 1230
Sun Valley ID
USA 83353
208-726-3358
Mr. Olin Gardner

Idaho Wilderness Camps
Box 1516
Salmon ID
USA 83467
208-756-2850
Mr. Garry Merritt

Indian Creek Ranch
Route 2, Box 105
North Fork ID
USA 83466
Salmon Operator
Ask For 24F211
Mr. Jack W. Briggs

Juniper Mountain Outfitters
Route 3, Box 50
Caldwell ID
USA 83605
208-454-1172
Mr. S. Meholchick

Keating, Earl R. Jr.
Box 3
Gibbonsville ID
USA 83463
208-865-2252

Lazy J Outfitters
Route 1
Kuna ID
USA 83634
208-922-5648
Mr. L. Jarrett

Little Wood River Outfitters
Box 425
Carey ID
USA 83320
208-823-4414
Mr. Robert Hennefer

Outfitters Directory: Hunting

North America

Lochsa River Outfitters
HC 75, Box 98
Kooskia ID
USA 83539
208-926-4149
Mr. Jack Nygaard

Lost Lake Outfitters
HCR 66, Box 226
Kooskia ID
USA 83539
208-926-4988
Mr. A. Latch

MacKay Bar
3190 Airport Way
Boise ID
USA 83705
800-635-5336
208-344-1881
Mr. R. Eardley

Meadow Creek Outfitters
Route 2, Box 264
Kooskia ID
USA 83530
208-926-4759
Ms. Cheryl Bransford

Merritt's Saddlery
P.O. Box 1516
Salmon ID
USA 83467
208-756-4170
Mr. Garry Merritt

Middle Fork Ranch Inc.
Box 7594
Boise ID
USA 83707
415-329-0260
Mr. Michael A. Szwek

Moose Creek Outfitters
Box 1181
Orofino ID
USA 83544
208-476-5227
Mr. Richard Norris

Moyie River Outfitters
(Sweet's Guide Service)
HCR 85, Box 54
Bonners Ferry ID
USA 83805
208-267-2108
Mr. Stanley A. Sweet

Mystic Saddle Ranch
Box 0
Stanley ID
USA 83340
208-774-3591
Mr. Jeff Bitton

Norman Guth Inc.
Box D
Salmon ID
USA 83467
208-756-3279

Paradise Outfitters
HCR 11, Box 74
Kamiah ID
USA 83536
208-935-0859
Mr. Rich Armiger

Pioneer Mountain Outfitters
Route 2, Box 5476
Twin Falls ID
USA 83301
208-734-3679
Mr. Thomas Proctor

Potts, Stanley
Outfitter
Box 1122
Hailey ID
USA 83333
208-788-4584

R & R Outdoors, Inc.
2755 Aspen Cove
Meridian ID
USA 83642
208-888-4676
Mr. Robert D. Black

Red River Corrals
Star Route, Box 18
Elk City ID
USA 83525
208-842-2228
Mr. A. George

Red Woods Outfitter
HC 2, Box 580
Pollock ID
USA 83547
208-628-3673
Mr. N.F. Woods

Renshaw, Jim
Star Route, Box 115
Kooskia ID
USA 83539
208-935-2829

Revell Enterprises
Box 674
Soda Springs ID
USA 83276
208-547-3016
Mr. P.K. Revell

Rivers Navigation
Box 1223
Lewiston ID
USA 83501
208-743-4800
Mr. W. Beamer

Robson, Dale R.
Box 44
Felt ID
USA 83424
208-456-2861

S & S Outfitters
912 Burrell
Lewiston ID
USA 83501
208-746-3569
Mr. David Bream

Salmon Meadows Lodge
Outfitter & Guides
HC 75, Box 3410
New Meadows ID
USA 83654
208-347-2357
Mr. Jim Thrash

Salmon River Lodge Inc.
Box 348
Jerome ID
USA 83338
208-324-3553
Mr. David Giles

Sawtooth Wilderness
Outfitters and Guides
730 W. Greenhurst
Nampa ID
USA 83651
208-466-8323
Mr. Leo V. Jarvis

Seal, Ray
Busterback Ranch
Ketchum ID
USA 83340
208-788-4809
208-774-2217

Selway Lodge
Star Route, Iron Creek
Salmon ID
USA 83467
208-894-2451
Mr. Rick (Ma) Hussey

Outfitters Directory: Hunting

North America

Seven Devils Outfitters, Inc.
P.O. Box 712
Riggins ID
USA 83549
208-628-3478
208-344-6600 TelRa
Mr. Bob Sentor

Seven Devils Outfitters Inc.
Box 487
McCall ID
USA 83638
208-634-7000

Sevey Guide Service Inc.
Box 1527
Sun Valley ID
USA 83353
208-774-2200
Mr. Bob Sevey

Shattuck Creek Ranch
and Outfitters
Box 165
Elk River ID
USA 83827
208-826-3284
208-826-3405
Mr. Andre Molsee

Shepp Ranch
Box 5446
Boise ID
USA
208-343-7729
Ms. Virginia Hopfenbeck

Sixty-Two (62) Ridge
Outfitters and Guides
4239 Old Ahsahka Grade
Ahsahka ID
USA 83520
208-476-7148
Mr. K.L. Smith

St. Joe Outfitters and Guides
HCR 1, Box 43-C
Harrison ID
USA 83833
208-689-3528
Mr. Ed Hunt

Stovers Outfitters
Box 604
Council ID
USA 83612
208-253-4352
Mr. John H. Stover

Sulphur Creek Ranch
7153 W. Emerald
Boise ID
USA 83704
208-377-1188
Mr. Tom Allegrezza

Sun Valley
Wilderness Outfitters
P.O. Box 303
Sun Valley ID
USA 83353
208-622-5019 Bus.
208-726-9449 Res.
Mr. R.J. Lewy

Taylor Ranch Outfitters
Box 398
Challis ID
USA 83226
208-879-4718
Con and Tina Hourihan

Teton Ranch
Box 1760
Tetonia ID
USA 83452
208-456-2896
Mr. Albert Tilt

Trapper Creek Outfitters
Triple T Ranch
Cascade ID
USA 83611
Mr. Anthony J. Popp Jr.

Triple O Outfitters
Box 21
Pierce ID
USA 83546
208-464-2349
208-464-2761
Mr. Harlan Opdahl

War Eagle Outfitter and
Guides
HC 61, Box 1009
Malta ID
USA 83342
208-645-2455
Mr. Ken Jafek

Weitas Creek Outfitters
Route 2, Box 115C
Potlatch ID
USA 83855
208-875-1190
208-875-0450
Mr. Steve Jones

Whitewater Outfitters
Salmon River Air Route
Cascade ID
USA 83611
208-382-4336
Mr. Lester West

Whitten Guide Service
Box 498
Riggins ID
USA 83549
208-628-3862
Mr. Harvey Whitten

Wilderness Recreation
Outfitter
1376 Walenta Drive
Moscow ID
USA 83843
208-882-5367
Mr. Harry Vaughn

York, Wally and Son Inc.
Box 319
Elk City ID
USA 83525
208-842-2367
Mr. W. Travis York

Montana

Bar 44 Outfitters and
Guide School
Box 493
Hamilton MT
USA 59840
406-363-3522
Mr. J.V. Rose

Bassett, Al
Box 4
Melstone MT
USA 59054
406-358-2360
Mr. A. Bassett

Beartooth
Plateau Outfitters
Box 28
Roberts MT
USA 59070
406-445-2293
Mr. R.L. Wright

Big Sky Pack Trips
Box 15
Stanford MT
USA 59479
406-566-2486
Mr. M.G. Pride

Outfitters Directory: Hunting

North America

Blue Rock Outfitters
Tongue River Stage
Miles City MT
USA 59301
Mr. K. Hughes

Broken Hart Ranch
Gallatin
Gateway MT
USA 59730
406-763-4279

Buckhorn Ranch, Inc.
Box 84
Eureka MT
USA 59917
406-889-3762
Mr. H.T. Workman

Bull Buffalo Outfitters
Box 658-B
Emigrant MT
USA 59027
406-848-7570
Mr. L. Britton

Cayuse Outfitters, Inc.
P.O. Box 1218
Livingston MT
USA 59047
406-222-3168
Mr. Larry Lahren

Crow Creek Outfitters
and Guides
Box 5
Toston MT
USA 59643
406-266-3742
Mr. M. Parsons

DL Elk Outfitters, Inc.
282 Ten Mile Road
Cascade MT
USA 59421
406-468-2642 LeV
406-452-4927 Bib
Dennis LeVeque or
Oren Biberdorf

DN&3 Outfitters
R.R. #1, Box 1602
Lewiston MT
USA 59457
406-538-8591
Mr. & Mrs. E. Snyder

Elk Valley Game Ranch
Box 430
Hardin MT
USA 59034
406-665-1215
Mr. Stan Hall

Hidden Valley Ranch
Augusta MT
USA 59410
406-562-3622
Mr. A. Weikum

Hole In The Wall Lodge
Box 134
Alberton MT
USA 59820
406-728-5203
Mr. Jeffry Freeman

Horse Creek Outfitters
Route 1, Box 667 (S-6)
Emmigrant MT
USA 59027
406-848-7144

Jack Atcheson & Sons, Inc.
3210 Ottawa Street
Butte MT
USA 59701
406-782-2382

Malson, Jerry
Star Route 2, Box 246
Trout Creek MT
USA 59874
406-847-5582

McAfee Outfitting
Route 1
Yaak River Ranch
Troy MT
USA 59935
406-295-4880
Mr. Bill McAfee

McDonough, N.L.
& Sons
Wolf Creek MT
USA 59648
406-235-4205

Montana Adventure Trips
West Fork Route
Darby MT
USA 59829
406-821-3763
Mr. K. Allaman

Montana Wilderness
Outfitters
4420 Watt Lane
Stevensville MT
USA 59870
406-777-3673
Mr. D. Kozub

Monte's Guiding and
Mountain Outfitting
16 North Fork Road
Townsend MT
USA 59644
406-266-3515
Mr. LaM. J. Schnur

North Star Outfitters
Box 65
Darby MT
USA 59829
406-821-3110
Mr. Ken Wolfinbarger

Point of Rocks Guest Ranch
Route 1, Box 680
Emigrant MT
USA 59027
406-333-4361
406-848-7278

Rock N' H Packers
West Fork, Route 1
Darby MT
USA 59829
406-821-3815
Mr. R.L. Stewart

Ron Mills Outfitting
Box 2
Augusta MT
USA 59410
406-562-3335

Rugg, Ray
Route 1, Box 58-G
St. Ignatius MT
USA 59865
406-745-4160

Running Creek Ranch
Box 509
Hamilton MT
USA 59840
208-382-4336
Mr. Edward Houghton

Saddle Mountain
Outfitting Co., Ltd.
P.O. Box 286
Hamilton MT
USA 59840
406-363-2356
Mr. J. Spear

Selway Magruder Outfitter
Box 135
Corvallis MT
USA 59828
406-961-4323
Don Habel and Sons

Outfitters Directory: Hunting

North America

Story Cattle Company
& Outfitting
Box 55
Emigrant MT
USA 59027
406-333-4739
Mr. Mike Story

Sun Canyon Lodge
Box 327
Augusta MT
USA 59410
406-562-3654
Mr. Lee Carlbom

Triple Tree Ranch
5480 Sourdough Road
Bozeman MT
USA 59715
406-587-4821
406-587-8513
Mr. B. Myers

Wildlife Outfitters
Guest Ranch
992 Pleasant View Drive
Victor MT
USA 59875
406-642-3262
406-642-3462
Jack and Shirley Wemple

WW Outfitters
Box 507
Darby MT
USA 59829
Mr. B. White

Yellowater Outfitters
P.O. Box 836
Grass Range MT
USA 59032
406-428-2195
Mr. R. Olsen

Yellowstone Outfitters
15100B Rocky Mtn. Road
Belgrade MT
USA 59714
406-388-4463

Twisted Pine Ranch
Box 84
Merriman NE
USA 69218
308-684-3482
Mr. K. Moreland

Oregon

BR Guide Service
Kiamath Falls OR
USA
503-882-1549 BMcD
503-884-2626 RA
Brooks McDowell or Russ
Altenburg

Cabin Creek Outfitters
P.O. Box 308
Stayton OR
USA 97383
503-581-4600

Joe Miller Guide Service
94771 Indian Creek Rd.
Gold Beach OR
USA 97444
503-247-6762
503-247-6067

North-West Hunting
Consultants
70744 Apiary Rd., Dept. SC
Rainier OR
USA 97048
503-556-9661
Mr. Duane Bernard

Old Oregon
Land and Livestock
P.O. Box 373
Pendleton OR
USA 97801
503-443-6861

South Dakota

Fair Chase Adventures
Box 630
Piedmont SD
USA 57769
800-843-8800
Ext. 22
Mr. Bo Hauer

Sioux Land Hunting Inc.
R.R. #1, Box 64
Naples SD
USA 57271
605-628-2987 RH
605-628-2200 GS
Mr. Rick Holiday

Washington

Bolwes, Ed
7022 West Fourth
Kennewick WA
USA 99336

Caswell, Jess
P.O. Box 432
Montesano WA
USA 98563
206-249-5687

Klineburger
Worldwide Travel
3627 1st Avenue South
Seattle WA
USA 98134
206-343-9699
Mr. C. Klineburger

St. Joe Hunting and
Fishing Camp Inc.
10405 Newport Hwy.
Spokane WA
USA 99218
509-467-5971
Mr. Don E. Dixon

Wyoming

AA Outfitters
Big Piney WY
USA 83113
307-276-3244
Mr. R.W. Ball

Absaroka Ranch
Fremont County, Star Route
Dubois WY
USA 82513
307-455-2275
Mr. Rbt. Betts, Jr.

Adams, T.T.
Box 2470
Jackson WY
USA 83001
307-733-2961

Allen Brothers Outfitting
Box 243
Lander WY
USA 82520
307-332-2995
Mr. J. Allen

Arrowhead Outfitters
P.O. Box 3252
Jackson WY
USA 83001
307-733-5223
Mr. Robert B. Lowe

Astle Hunting Camp
Box 121
Bedford WY
USA 83112
307-883-2750
Mr. F.B. Astle

Outfitters Directory: Hunting

North America

Atkinson, Dale
Box 108
Moran WY
USA 83013
307-543-2442

Bald Mountain Outfitters
P.O. Box 754, Sublette Co.
Pinedale WY
USA 82941
307-367-6539
Mr. T.A. Pollard

Barkhurst, Dick
Star Route, Box 13
Saratoga WY
USA 82331
307-327-5350
Mr. D. Barkhurst

Battle Mountain Outfitters
1235 Johnson Avenue
Thermopolis WY
USA 82443
307-864-2620
Mr. J.W. Lumley

Bear Creek Hunting Camp
Box 623, Fremont County
Crowheart WY
USA 82512
307-486-2215
Mr. F.G. Fox

Bear Creek Hunting Camp
Box 222, Teton County
Wilson WY
USA 83014
307-733-4314
Mr. P.G. Gilroy

Bear Track Outfitters
Kaycee Rt., Box 2D,
Johnson Co.
Buffalo WY
USA 82834
307-684-2528
307-684-5804
Mr. Peter J. Dube

Beaver Creek Outfitters
Box 673
Big Piney WY
USA 83113
307-276-5372
307-276-3748
Mr. K. Manning

Bernard, Tim
Wildrose Ranch
P.O. Box 737
Dubois WY
USA 82513

Big Horn Mountain Outfitters
5060 Coffeen, Sheridan Co.
Sheridan WY
USA 82801
307-672-2813
Mr. T. Johnson

Billings, John R.
Box 3127
Cody WY
USA 82414
307-587-5609

BJ Outfitters
5510 Alcova Rt.
Casper WY
USA 82604
307-472-7956 Holli
307-577-1176 Ellis
Mr. Hollingsworth or
Mr. Ellison

Black Mountain Outfitters
412 E. Burkitt, Sheridan Co.
Sheridan WY
USA 82801
307-674-7369
Mr. J. Yeager

Blizzard Creek Trophy Hunts
Box 2015, Park County
Cody WY
USA 82414
307-587-5011
Mr. Bill Smith

Bolten Ranch Outfitters
7000 Valley View Place
Cheyenne WY
USA 82009
307-637-6017
307-635-8066
Mr. John Anderson

Bondurant Creek
Hunting Camp
1515 South Park Rt.
Jackson WY
USA 83001
307-733-5069
Mr. E.G. Wampler

Boulder Lake Lodge
P.O. Box 2200
Pinedale WY
USA 82941
307-367-2961
Mr. Kim Bright

Boulder Lake Ranch
P.O. Box 725, Sublette Co.
Pinedale WY
USA 82941
307-367-4627
Mr. G.G. Petersen

Box K Ranch
Teton County
Moran WY
USA 83013
307-543-2407
Mr. W. Korn

Box R Ranch
Box 23, Sublette County
Cora WY
USA 82925
307-367-2291
Mr. I. Lozier

Box Y Lodge
Route 1, Lincoln County
Afton WY
USA 83110
307-886-5459
Mr. K. Clark

Boxelder Ranch
Box 3720
Ten Sleep WY
USA 82442
Mr. M. Bush

Boysen Outfitters
Box 66
Shoshoni WY
USA 82649
307-876-2636
Mr. B. Weaver

Bud Nelson's
Big Game Outfitters
P.O. Box 409
Jackson WY
USA 83001
307-733-2843

C.J. Outfitter/Guide
1010 S. Washington
Casper WY
USA 82601
307-235-1975
Mr. J. Dye

Cabin Creek Outfitters, Inc.
1313 Lane 10, Route 1
Powell WY
USA 82435
307-754-9279
Mr. D. Wiltse

Outfitters Directory: Hunting

North America

Castle Rock Ranch
412 Road 6, N-S, Park Co.
Cody WY
USA 82414
307-587-2076
Mr. J. Tilden

Cleav. Creek Outfitter
P.O. Box 177, Sheridan Co.
Clearmont WY
USA 82835
307-758-4388
Mr. R.R. Smith

Cloud Peak Outfitters
P.O. Box 4032
Casper WY
USA 82604
307-265-0334
Kenneth McCants or
Paul Schukman

Cole, Dick
Route 1, Box 1779
Cody WY
USA 82414
307-587-2026

Coulter Creek Outfitters
Box 504
Jackson WY
USA
307-733-6557
Mr. B. Johnson

Coy's Yellow Creek Outfitters
P.O. Box 3055, Park County
Cody WY
USA 82414
307-587-6944
Mr. B.J. Coy

Crittenden, Paul
P.O. Box 185
Sublette County
Bondurant WY
USA 82922
307-733-6740

Cross Mill-Iron Ranch
Fremont County
Crowheart WY
USA 82512
307-486-2279
Mr. L.C. Miller

Crossed Sabres
Park County
Wapiti WY
USA 82450
307-587-3750
Mr. F.A. Norris

Crystal Creek Outfitters
Star Route, Box 44A
Jackson WY
USA 83001
307-733-6318
Mr. G. Puche

D. T. Outfitting
Box 891, Route 63
Lander WY
USA 82520
307-332-3123
Mr. R. Focht

Dan's Outfitting
5 Hill Drive
Wheatland WY
USA 82201
Mr. D. Artery

David Ranch
Sublette County
Daniel WY
USA 83115
307-859-8228
Mr. Melvin David

Deadman Creek Outfitters
P.O. Box 232
Alpine WY
USA 83128
307-654-7528
Mr. G. Fischer

Diamond D Ranch Outfitters
Box 211, Teton County
Moran WY
USA 83013
307-543-2479
Mr. R. Doty

Diamond J Outfitters
Box 1347, Carbon County
Saratoga WY
USA 82331
307-326-8259
Mr. J. Stuemke

Dodge Creek Ranch
402 Tunnel Road, Albany Co.
Rock River WY
USA 82083
307-322-2345
Mr. J. Kennedy

Dube, Ron
R.R. #1, Box 95,
Johnson Co.
Buffalo WY
USA 82834
307-684-5464

Dvarishkis, Ramul
Hot Springs County
Hamilton Dome WY
USA 82427
307-867-2262

East Table Creek
Hunting Camp
P.O. Box 2277, Campbell Co.
Gillette WY
USA 82716
307-682-4196
Mr. F. Donaldson

Elk Mountain
Safari, Inc.
P.O. Box 188
Saratoga WY
USA 82331
307-326-8773
Mr. E. Beattie

Elk Mountain Outfitters
Wheatland WY
USA 82201
307-322-3220
Mr. M.J. Wakkuri

Finley Ranch
Fremont County
Dubois WY
USA 82513
307-455-2494
Mr. O.F. Finley

Fir Creek Ranch
Box 190, Teton County
Moran WY
USA 83013
307-543-2416
Mr. P. Finch

Fleming, Warren
Box 2033, Teton County
Jackson WY
USA 83001
307-733-2493

Flitner, Dave
Packing & Outfitting
Greybull WY
USA 82426
307-765-2961

Flying H Ranch
598 Hunter Creek Road
Cody WY
USA 82414
307-587-2089

Outfitters Directory: Hunting

North America

Flying V Hunting Lodge
Lic. Outfitters & Guides
P.O. Box 158
Newcastle WY
USA 82701
307-746-2096

Gardner, Low
Lincoln County
Smoot WY
USA 83126
307-886-5665

Garst, Russell
Box 400, Trailcreek Road
Weston WY
USA 82731
307-682-0119

Gibbs, Donald J.
Box 216, Park County
Cody WY
USA 82414
307-587-4198

Grand & Sierra Outfitters
Box 312
Encampment WY
USA 82325
307-327-5200
Mr. G. Knotwell

Grand Slam
Outfitters, Inc.
Box 1098
Saratoga WY
USA 82331
307-326-5508
Mr. M. Condict

Grassy Lake Outfitters
Box 853, Teton Co.
Jackson WY
USA 83001
307-733-6779
Mr. B.J. Wilson

Green River Outfitters
P.O. Box 727
Pinedale WY
USA 82941
307-367-2416
Mr. Wm. A. Webb

Greer, Randy C.
404 Prairieview Drive
Gillette WY
USA 82716
307-682-5781

Grey Horse Outfitter
P.O. Box 428,
Natrona County
Mills WY
USA 82644
307-265-5669
Mr. Morris L. Carter, Jr.

Greybull River Outfitters
Box 1431
Evanston WY
USA 82930
307-789-7126
Mr. C. Griffith

Grizzly Ranch
Park County
Cody WY
USA 82414
307-587-3966
Mr. R. Felts

Haderlie Outfitting and
Guide Service
Box 126
Freedom WY
USA 83120
208-873-2353
Mr. Vaughn Haderlie

Hagen, Duaine K.
153 Hidden Valley Road
Cody WY
USA 82414
307-587-5090

Heart 6 Ranch
Box 70, Teton County
Moran WY
USA 83013
307-543-2477
Mr. C. Garnick

Hidden Basin Outfitters
P.O. Box 7182
Jackson WY
USA 83001
307-733-7980
Mr. N. Meeks

High Country Outfitters
Rt. 1, Box 33,
Big Horn County
Deaver WY
USA 82421
307-664-2241
Mr. R. Olson

Highland Meadows Ranch
Fremont County
Dubois WY
USA 82513
Mr. J. Detimore

Hollingsworth, Wm.
5510 Alcova Route
Casper WY
USA 82604
307-472-7956

Horse Creek Ranch
Box 3878
Jackson WY
USA 83001
307-733-6566
Mr. Ray Billings

Indian Creek Outfitters
Box 2882, Teton County
Jackson WY
USA 83001
307-733-9207
Mr. B. Moyer

J & B Outfitters
Box 4246
1812 Fremont, Natrona Co.
Casper WY
USA 82604
307-237-5363
James Fritz or Bud Currah

Jackson Hole Country
Outfitters
Box 20102
Jackson WY
USA 83112
307-883-2999
Mr. M. Jones

Jensen Hunting Camp
Route 1, Lincoln Co.
Afton WY
USA 83110
307-886-3401
Mr. K.C. Jensen

Johnson, Dean
Box 1535, Park County
Cody WY
USA 82414
307-587-4072

Llano Outfitters
630 Trigood Drive,
Natrona Co.
Casper WY
USA 826009
307-235-4865
Mr. J. Savini

M.F. Hunting
Box 724, Teton County
Jackson WY
USA 83001
307-733-2271
Mr. L. Feuz

Outfitters Directory: Hunting

North America

Mankin Wildlife
Box 1239, Campbell County
Gillette WY
USA 82716
307-682-3007
Mr. R. Mankin

McNeel & Sons Inc.
Rural Route, Teton County
Alpine WY
USA 83128
307-654-7643
Mr. M. McNeel

Merritt, Lamont
Route 1, Lincoln County
Afton WY
USA 83110
307-886-5508

Metzger, Dean
Box 734
Dubois WY
USA 82513
307-455-2938

Morning Creek Outfitter
Box 101, Park County
Cody WY
USA 82414
307-587-4647
Mr. B. Reid

P Cross Bar Outfitters
8586A N. Hiway 14-16,
Campbell Co.
Gillette WY
USA 82716
307-682-3994
Mr. M. Scott

Page, Dick
1625 Holly, Natrona Co.
Casper WY
USA 82604
307-237-7866

Pass Creek Outfitters
Box 14, Fremont County
Arapahoe WY
USA 82510
307-856-6812
Mr. R.K. Miller

Pennoyer, Stanley
Owl Creek Route,
Hot Springs Co.
Thermopolis WY
USA 82443
307-867-2407

Petersen, Charlie Jr.
Box 1074, Teton County
Jackson WY
USA 83001
307-733-3805

Peterson, Everett D.
P.O. Box 1166, Lincoln Co.
Afton WY
USA 83110
307-886-9693

Pilgrim Creek Hunting Camp
Box 1443, Teton County
Jackson WY
USA 83001
307-733-3476
Mr. J. Davis

Platt, Ron
Guides/Outfitters
Star Route, Box 49,
Carbon Co.
Encampment WY
USA 82325
307-327-5539

Ponderosa Lodge
P.O. Box 832, Sublette Co.
Pinedale WY
USA 82941
307-367-2516
Mr. G. Weiss

Powder River Outfitter
603 Sourdough, Box 37A
Buffalo WY
USA 82834
307-684-2436
Mr. J.P. Francis

Rafter B Outfitters
R.R. #1, Johnson County
Buffalo WY
USA 82834
307-684-2793
Mr. L.R. Brannian

Rand Creek Outfitter
P.O. Box 128
Wapiti WY
USA 82450
307-587-5077
Mr. D. Blevins

Randle, Don
Box 911, Fremont County
Dubois WY
USA 82513
307-455-2351

Red Desert Outfitters
P.O. Box 1201
Green River WY
USA 82935
307-875-6199
Mr. V. Dana

Rimrock Ranch
2728 Northfork Route
Cody WY
USA 82414
307-587-3970
Mr. G. Fales

Robinson, William
P.O Box 1124, Teton Co.
Jackson WY
USA 83001
307-733-3308

Rockin DBL R Outfit
2760 Robertson, RD38
Casper WY
USA 82604
307-234-7732
Mr. L.F. Beekley

Rose, Don
Box 352, Fremont Co.
Dubois WY
USA 82513
307-455-2467

Rough Country Outfitters
P.O. Box 973, Converse Co.
Glenrock WY
USA 82637
307-436-2304
Mr. J.D. Schell

RR Haecker Outfitter
Box 818, Teton County
Jackson WY
USA 83001
307-733-6195
Mr. R.R. (Randy) Haecker

S & S Outfitter/Guide Service
1818 S. Washington
Casper WY
USA 82601
307-266-4229
Mr. S. Gilliland

Saddle Pocket Ranch
143 Mazet Road,
Fremont Co.
Riverton WY
USA 82501
307-856-1720
Mr. G. Fuechsel

Outfitters Directory: Hunting

North America

Safari Outfitters
16 Musser Rd.
Cody WY
USA 82414
307-587-3888
Ms. Gretchen Stark

Sand Creek Ranch Outfitters
General Delivery
Alcova WY
USA 82620
Mr. J. Collins

Sanger, Chuck
Box 745, Carbon County
Saratoga WY
USA 82331
307-326-5696

Savage Run Outfitter
49 Pahlow Land, Albany Co.
Laramie WY
USA 82070
307-745-5958
Mr. Jim Talbott

Sheep Mesa Outfitters
121 Road 20
Cody WY
USA 82414
307-587-4014 RG
307-587-4305 DG
Dale Good or Ron Good

Shoemaker, Les
C M Ranch - Fremont County
Dubois WY
USA 82513

Siggins, Don
Southfork Route, Park County
Cody WY
USA 82414

Silver Star Ranch
148 Road, Route 6
Cody WY
USA 82414
307-587-2036
Mr. Bob Loran

Skinner Brothers
Box B, Sublette County
Pinedale WY
USA 82835
307-758-4388
Mr. O. Skinner

Snow, Hank
Sublette County
Boulder WY
USA 82923
307-367-4649

South Fork Expeditions
391 Hunter Creek Road,
Park Co.
Cody WY
USA 82414
307-587-6275
Mr. J. De Sarro

Spear-O-Wigwam Ranch
Box 328, Sheridan County
Story WY
USA 82842
307-683-2226
307-674-4496
Mr. A. MacCarty

Spearhead Ranch
3493 Ross Road, Route 3
Douglas WY
USA 82633
307-358-2694
Mr. F.N. Moore

Spotted Horse Ranch
Teton County
Jackson WY
USA 83001
307-733-2097
Mr. Dick Bess

Star Valley Outfitters
P.O. Box 143, Lincoln County
Smoot WY
USA 83126
307-886-9585
Mr. R. Clark

Stearns Outfitting
51 Red Rock Drive
Douglas WY
USA 82633
307-358-6580
Mr. G.R. Stearns

Stephens, Press
P.O. Box 29,
Big Horn County
Shell WY
USA 82441
307-765-4377

Stetter General Outfitter
P.O. Box 695, Fremont Co.
Dubois WY
USA 82513
307-455-2725
Mr. L.F. Stetter

Stevenson Outfitting
940 North Center,
Natrona Co.
Casper WY
USA 82601
307-237-8176
Mr. J. Stevenson

Stilson, Keith
Box 1885, Teton County
Jackson WY
USA 83001

Sweetwater Gap Ranch
Box 26, Sweetwater Co.
Rock Springs WY
USA 82901
307-362-2798
Mr. B. Wilmetti

Sweetwater Outfitters
P.O. Box 4188, Natrona Co.
Casper WY
USA 82604
307-266-1424
Mr. R. Dennis

T Lazy T Outfitting
P.O. Box 1288, Teton Co.
Jackson WY
USA 83001
307-733-4481
Mr. T. Toolson

Table Mountain Outfitters
P.O. Box 2714-SCI
Cheyenne WY
USA 82003
307-632-6352

Tass, Leo
K C Route, Box 14,
Johnson Co.
Buffalo WY
USA 82834

Taylor, Glenn B.
Box 37, Teton County
Kelly WY
USA 83011
307-733-4851

Taylor, Ridge W.
Outfitters
P.O. Box 2356, Teton County
Jackson WY
USA 83001
307-733-9041
Mr. R.W. Taylor

Outfitters Directory: Hunting

North America

Teton Country Outfitters
P.O. Box 7434
Jackson WY
USA 83001
307-733-6817
Mr. D. Lloyd

Teton Outfitters
Star Route, Box 355
Wilson WY
USA 83014
307-733-5414
Mr. E.A. Linn

Teton Trail Rides, Inc.
P.O. Box 1350, Teton Co.
Jackson WY
USA 83001
307-733-6409
Mr. C. Rudd

Teton Wilderness Outfitting
P.O. Box 442, Sheridan Co.
Ranchester WY
USA 82839
307-655-2451
Mr. N. Vance

The Last Resort
Box 38, Sublette County
Daniel WY
USA 83115
307-859-8294
Mr. D. Roberts

Thompson, Dick
Box 17, Sublette County
Cora WY
USA 82925
307-367-4551

Thorofare Outfitting
P.O. Box 604
Cody WY
USA 82414
307-587-5929
Mr. D. Schmalz

Thunder Ridge Outfitters
849 South Spruce
Casper WY
USA 82601
307-237-3329
307-266-1919
Mr. J. Galles

Timberline Outfitter
1202 West, 32 Street
Cheyenne WY
USA 82001
307-635-7288
Mr. C. Oceanak

Tjomsland, Cy
Fremont County
Dubois WY
USA 82513

Trapper Galloway Ranch
Box 1222, Big Horn County
Shell WY
USA 82441
307-765-2971
Mr. F.K. Smith, Jr.

Triangle C Ranch
P.O. Box 691, Fremont Co.
Dubois WY
USA 8213
307-455-2225
Mr. J.L. Pavlik

Triangle X Ranch
Teton County
Moose WY
USA 83012
307-733-3612
307-733-2183
Don and Harold Turner

Triple X Ranch
Park County
Cody WY
USA 82414
307-587-2031
Mr. S. Siggins

Turpin Meadow Ranch
Box 48
Moran WY
USA 83013
Mr. G. Wocicki

Two Ocean Pass Outfitters
P.O. Box 2322
Jackson WY
USA 83001
307-733-5962
Mr. G.A. Rickman

Two Ocean Pass Outfitter
P.O. Box 472
Wright WY
USA 82732
307-464-0189
Mr. J. Robidoux

Ullery, Brad J.
3045 East 4th St.,
Natrona Co.
Casper WY
USA 82604
307-233-5453

Ullery, Dick
Box 1218, Natrona County
Casper WY
USA 82602
307-235-5453

Ullery, Harold
Box 9680
3045 East 4th St.,
Natrona Co.
Casper WY
USA 82609
307-265-9051

Vehnekamp, Bill
267 Lwr. Southfork Road
Cody WY
USA 82414
307-587-4063

Wallace Brothers Outfitters
Box 3366, Teton County
Jackson WY
USA 83001
307-733-2591
Mr. J.T. Wallace

Wilderness Outfitters
P.O. Box 1072
Dubois WY
USA 82513
307-455-2463
307-235-1759
Mr. R. Hansen

Wilderness Trails
Box 1113, Teton County
Jackson WY
USA 83001
307-733-9051
Mr. G. Clover

Winter, John R.
Outfitter & Guide
Route 1, Box 1922
Cody WY
USA 82414
307-587-4021

Wolf Mountain Outfitters
Route 1
Afton WY
USA 83110
307-886-9317
Mr. G. Azevedo

Wolverine Creek Outfitter
P.O. Box 9, Sublette County
Pinedale WY
USA 82941
307-367-2580
Mr. M. Nystrom, Sr.

Outfitters Directory: Hunting

North America

Wyoming Peak Outfitters
Afton WY
USA 83110
307-886-3936 Afton
307-279-3344 Cokev
Mr. Billy D. Peterson

Wyoming Safari, Inc.
P.O. Box 1126
Saratoga WY
USA 82331
307-327-5530
307-327-5502
Mr. W.G. Condict

Wyoming Wilderness
2051 Road 11, Park County
Powell WY
USA 82435
307-754-4320
Mr. Jake Clark

Wyoming Wilderness
Outfitters
Box 4311, Natrona County
Casper WY
USA 82604
307-235-4511
Mr. D. Simpson

Wyoming Wilderness
Outfitters
1051 Road 11, Route 3
Powell WY
USA 82435
307-754-4320
Mr. J. Clark

Yellowstone Country
Outfitters
32 Creek Lane, Park County
Cody WY
USA 82414
307-587-3596
Mr. M.C. Cosat

Z K Outfitters
P.O. Box 284, Fremont Co.
Dubois WY
USA 82513
307-455-2210
Mr. G.J. Rice

Unites States
South East

Florida

Argentina Hunting
and Fishing
P.O. Box 1349
Big Pine Key FL
USA 33149
305-554-8875
Mr. R. Ortega

Caravelle Ranch
Star Route 19, Box 168
Palatka FL
USA 32077
904-325-0032
Mr. J.W. Gorab

Dixie Wildlife Safaris
4431 Walk-in-Water Rd.
Lake Wales FL
USA 33853
813-696-3300
Mr. M. Acreman

Eric Wagner Safaris Inc.
2065 NE 125th Terrace Road
Silver Springs FL
USA 32688
904-625-2100

G. & W. Adventures
822 3rd Avenue South
Tierra Verde FL
USA 33715
813-866-3189
813-867-0893
Mr. B. Grant

Issacs, Bill
P.O. Box 79
Everglades City FL
USA 33929

Pinney, Richard
Box 14318
Gainnesville FL
USA 32604
904-378-3000

Safari Consultants Inc.
Box 14318
Gainnesville FL
USA 32604
904-378-3000

Safari De Colombia
8166 150th Place North
Palm Beach Gardens FL
USA 33410
305-747-8230

Sohrada Safaris
1455 Tolson Rd.
Deland FL
USA 32720
904-738-3295
Mr. B. Agnew

Trophy Hunter Safaris Inc.
Suite 1407,
1000 Quayside Terrace
Miami FL
USA 33138
305-893-1162
Ms. B. Jones Levitz

Voight, Robin W.
12 North Lake
First Ave. FL
USA 1710
011-672-5769

Georgia

Burnt Pine Plantation Inc.
2250 Newmarket Pkwy.,
Suite 112
Marietta GA
USA 30067
404-953-0326
Ms. Cindy Robinson

Custom Hunts
404 Tripp Street
Americus GA
USA
800-223-4868
912-924-8318 Coll.

Professional Adventure
Consultants
404 Tripp Street
Americus GA
USA
800-223-4868

Louisianna

EWW Safari Innovators
Rt. 3, Box 258
Tallulah LA
USA 71282
318-574-1230
Mr. E.W. Williams

International Tours &
Expeditions
3749 Perkins Road
Baton Rouge LA
USA 70808
504-344-9476
800-222-0387

Outfitters Directory: Hunting

North America

Laguna Vista
P.O. Box 580
New Roads LA
USA 70760
504-638-8682(4048)
1-800-233-3985
Mr. D. Williams

Missouri

High Adventure Game
Ranch, Inc.
8330 Watson Road,
Suite 205
St. Louis MO
USA 63119
314-849-5700
314-894-3776

Rio Arriba Trophy Hunts
#11 Solano Circle, Gulf Hills
Ocean Springs MS
USA 39564
601-875-6888

Virginia

Abrams Creek Outfitters
P.O. Box 790,
140 North 21st St.
Purcellville VA
USA 22132
703-338-5848
Mr. G. Abrams

Nathan, Tink
P.O. Box NN
McLean VA
USA 22101

United States
South West

Arizona

Arizona Trophy Hunting
P.O. Box 1021
Flagstaff AZ
USA 86002
602-525-9206
Mr. L. Shelton

Coon, Gene
Guide Service
P.O. Box 1464
Showlow AZ
USA 85901
602-537-7164

James, Russel
P.O. Box 41
Lakeside AZ
USA 85929
602-368-5525

Kaibab Outfitters
P.O. Box 2642
Flagstaff AZ
USA 86003
602-774-5008
602-774-4318
Mr. B. Dixon

Miller Bros. Outfitters
AZ
USA
602-327-8673 CM
602-881-6541 MM
Chris and Mike Miller

Safari Club International
5151 East Broadway
Suite 1680
Tucson AZ
USA 85711
602-747-0260

Sportman's Adventures
10809 N. 99th Street
Scottsdale AZ
USA 85260
602-860-8835
602-991-9282
Mr. F. Romley

Sutherland, Charlie
P.O. Box 2737
Showlow AZ
USA 85901
602-537-2611

White Mountain
Apache Tribe
P.O. Box 220
Whiteriver AZ
USA 85941
Mr. P. Stago, Jr.

California

Bow 'n' Bore Ranch
P.O. Box 2102
Livermore CA
USA 94550
408-897-3262
Mr. S. Swart

Burrows Ranch, Inc.
c/o Bill Burrows
12250 Colyer Sprints Rd.
Red Bluff CA
USA 96080
916-529-1535

California Outfitters
5285 E. Kings Canyon Rd.,
#135
Fresno CA
USA 93727
209-456-0663 Res.
916-824-2850 Ranch
Mr. G. Flournoy, Jr.

CB Travel Service
877 Cowan Road
Burlingame CA
USA 94010
Mr. L. Bohner

Deel, Boyd B.
1228 Wooded Hills
San Jose CA
USA 19120PHA46

Destiny West Travel
P.O. Box 1188
Rosemead CA
USA 91770
818-307-5502

East Africa Safari
Consultants, Ltd.
8235 Soledad Canyon Road
Acton CA
USA 93510
805-268-0322
Mr. W. Dougherty

Handrich, Dave
6474 Stagecoach Road
Santa Barbara CA
USA 93105
805-964-2965

John Gibson Safaris
Dept. S.K.
4055 Wilshire Blvd.,
Suite 526
Los Angeles CA
USA 90010

Lainoff Robbins Safaris
4111 Illinois St.,
P.O. Box 40181
San Diego CA
USA 92104
619-283-1162

Matthew, Tom
3481 Lupine Drive
Redding CA
USA 96002
916-223-6424

Outfitters Directory: Hunting

North America

Multiple Use Managers, Inc.
P.O. Box L
West Point, CA
USA 95255
209-293-7087

Ngezi Safaris
12066 Horely Avenue
Downey CA
USA 90242
Mr. R. Comstock

Penland Guide Service
Box 303
Big Bend CA
USA 96011
916-337-6471
916-547-4952

Rancho San Lucas
Box 100
San Lucas CA
USA 93954
408-382-4321

Safaris Jacques Guin
1301 Rossmoyne Avenue
Glendale CA
USA 91207
818-246-6077
Mr. J. Perkins

Schmidt, Nessen
Box 105 - Oasis Rd.
King City CA
USA 93930
805-472-9165

Tony da Costa's Safari
Headquarters
P.O. Box 284
Lompoc CA
USA 93438
805-736-1098

Colorado

Challenge Outfitters
P.O. Box 5092
Steamboat Springs CO
USA 80477
303-879-0595
Mr. D. Elder

Cimarron Outfitters
& Packers School
72834 Kinikin Road
Montrose CO
USA 81401
303-249-7174
Mr. B. Lane

Colorado High
Guide Service
1759 S. Ironton
Aurora CO
USA 80012
303-751-9274
Mr. C. Benson

Cotton Gordon
Safaris Ltd.
Tarryall River Ranch
Lake George CO
USA 80827
303-748-3255

Fair Chase Safaris
1130 Main Avenue
Durango CO
USA 81301
1-800-243-9658
303-259-3831

Grizzly Creek Guide Services
2911 Four Corners Pk.
Grand Junction CO
USA 81503
Mr. T. Wood

High Plains Safaris
P.O. Box 0562
Hudson CO
USA 80642
303-659-5942

High Plains Safaris
P.O. Box 2053
Longmont CO
USA 80502
308-882-5555

Hofmann Hunting
Guide Service
61278 E. Monroe
Montrose CO
USA 81401
303-249-2363
303-249-9551
Mr. M. Hofmann

Horn Fork Guides
29178 County Rd. 361
Buena Vista CO
USA 81211
303-395-8363
Mr. Glen Roberts

International Adventures
Unlimited, Inc.
P.O. Box 1157
Gunnison CO
USA 81230
303-641-5369
Mr. M. Grosse

J/B Adventures & Safaris,
Inc., Suite 330N
6312 South Fiddler's
Green Circle
Englewood CO
USA 80111
303-771-0977

Little Creek Ranches
P.O. Box 171
Collbran CO
USA 81624
303-487-3321
303-241-7272
Mr. A.L. Baier

Lobo Outfitters
Rt. 2, Box 9A
Pagosa Springs CO
USA 81147
303-264-5546

Loncarich, Chris
Guide/Outfitter
950 R. Road
Mack CO
USA 81525

McLeod Outfitters
P.O. Box 132
Crawford CO
USA 81415
303-921-7731 TMcL
817-625-7261 CWhit
Tom McLeod or
Charles Whitmire

Mountain Mesa Safaris
P.O. Box 15836
Colorado Springs CO
USA 80935
303-597-4062
Mr. J. Snyder

Mountain West
Expeditions, Inc.
2558 E. Nichols Circle
Littleton CO
USA 80122
303-796-9635
Mr. T. Tietz

Quaking Aspen
Guides & Outfitters
P.O. Box 485
Gunnison CO
USA 81230
303-641-0529
Mr. D. Mapes

Outfitters Directory: Hunting

North America

Redwing Outfitters
P.O. Box 149
Gardner CO
USA 81040
303-746-2269

Saddle Mountain
Guide Service
Star Route
Crawford CO
USA 81415
303-921-3651
Mr. L. Zeldenthius

Sammons Bros.
Guides & Outfitters
Box 1346
Grand Junction CO
USA 81502
303-241-1183
303-244-9852

Slater Creek Outfitters
13761E Lehigh, Ste. A
Aurora CO
USA 80014
303-690-1017

The Taylor Ranch
P.O. Box 96
San Luis CO
USA 81152
303-672-3580
Mr. R.J. McGrath

Vadoma Safaris
P.O. Box 441
Hayden CO
USA 81639
303-276-3885
Mr. D. Gore

Vadoma Safaris Ltd.
545 Estes Street
Lakewood CO
USA 80226
303-237-2110
Mr. Rbt. Woodfill

Wapiti Outfitter & Guides
P.O. Box 932
Gunnison CO
USA 81230
303-641-2603
303-641-3220
Mr. J. Garfall

Waterways West, Ltd.
P.O. Box 40071
Grand Junction CO
USA 81507
303-241-8188
Mr. E. Glade

Hawaii

Hunting Adventures of Maui
645 B Kaupakalua Rd.
Haiku, Maui HI
USA 96708
808-572-8214
Mr. B. Caires

Nokaoi Outfitters
P.O. Box 556
Wailuku, Maui HI
USA 96793
Mr. R. DeRego

Kansas

Midwestern Hunting
Consultants
Route 1, Box 134
Baxter Springs KS
USA 66713
316-674-8863
Mr. K. Shira

New Mexico

Beaverhead Outfitters
Beaverhead Lodge-Ranch
Beaverhead Route
Magdalena NM
USA 87825
505-772-5795
505-772-5517
Mr. Jack Diamond

Black Range Guide
and Outfitting
P.O. Box 97
Winston NM
USA 87943
Mr. S. Carter

Cougar Mountain
Guide Service
P.O. Box 31
Corona NM
USA 88318
Mr. D. Dobbs

Hi Valley Outfitters
P.O. Box 776-A
Tres Piedras NM
USA 87577
505-758-2616

Johnson, Ross
Guide/Outfitter
P.O. Box 194
Hillsboro NM
USA 88042
505-895-5600

Mundy Ranch
Box 386
Cimarron NM
USA 87714
Mr. F. Sturges

Neal, Dirk
Outfitter
P.O. Box 193
Red River NM
USA 87558

New Mexico CS Ranch
Eagle Nest Dam
Eagle Nest NM
USA 87718
505-377-6521
505-377-6878
Mr. L. Brooks

Runnels Outfitter
Guide Service
Box 596
Capitan NM
USA 88316
Mr. R. Runnels

Stone, Preston
Guide/Outfitter
Box 484
Capitan NM
USA 88316

Trophy Adventures Ltd.
Mountain Route, Box 20
Jemez Springs NM
USA 87025
505-829-3897
Mr. R. Martin

Nevada

Agua Fria Guide Service
1001 S. Third St., Ste. 1
Las Vegas NV
USA 89101
Mr. Mike Bucks

Hurtado Desert Bighorn
Guide Service
8310 Fisher Avenue
Las Vegas NV
USA 89129
702-645-1855
Mr. M. Hurtado

Oklahoma

Neal Hunting Company
7901 So. Sheridan
Tulsa OK
USA 74133
918-492-1653

Outfitters Directory: Hunting

North America

Texoma Hunting
Wilderness Inc.
2301 Hidden Lake Dr.
Norman OK
USA 73069
405-329-8933

Texas

Adobe Lodge Hunting Camp
Route 5, Box 5055
San Angelo TX
USA 76901
915-949-6885
915-942-8040
Mr. S. Duncan

Dallas Safari Club
Twin Towers, Ste. 770S
8585 Stemmons
Dallas TX
USA 75247
214-630-1453

Game Conservation
International
Box 17444
San Antonio TX
USA 78217

Game Conservation
International
444 Fort Worth Club Bldg.
Fort Worth TX
USA 76102
817-335-1942
Mr. H. Tennison

Gilchrist, Dooley
Box 67
Spring Branch TX
USA 78070

Greenwood Valley Ranch
Rt. 1, Box 75
Mountain Home TX
USA 78058
512-683-3411
Mr. J. Hunt

High Sierra Outfitters
Rt. 2, Box 2042-A
Kempwer TX
USA 76539
512-556-2453
Mr. B. Glosson

Hoffmann, G.L.
Box 1458
Sonora TX
USA 76950

Hunters Africa
6 Desta Drive, Ste. 5800
Midland TX
USA 79705-5510
915-682-6324

Indianhead Ranch, Inc.
Safaris
R.R. #1, Box 2
Del Rio TX
USA 78840
512-775-6481

International Prof.
Hunters' Association
Box 17444
San Antonio TX
USA 78217
512-824-7509

Nunley Brothers Ranches
P.O. Box 308
Sabinal TX
USA 78881
512-988-2752

Outdoor Expeditions
4026 Westheimer
Houston TX
USA 77027
713-621-7342
Mr. D. Petersen

Plemons, Scott D.
801 W. Vickery
Ft. Worth TX
USA 76104
817-332-1598

Real Hunting
Box 536 WS
Marfa TX
USA 79843
915-467-2902

Rio Grande Rancho
11719 Raindrop
San Antonio TX
USA 78216
512-342-0430
512-947-3647
Jeffrey Myers and Lee Taylor

Safari South
Sporting International
Ste. 504,
7701 Wilshire Place Dr.
Houston TX
USA 77040
713-785-6681
713-744-3527

Seven Seventy-Seven Ranch
P.O. Box 458069
San Antonio TX
USA 78280-8069
512-675-1408

Tadlock, Paul
Rt. 8, Box 850
New Braunfels TX
USA 78130
512-625-4346

Texotic Wildlife Inc.
P.O. Box 181
Mountain Home TX
USA 78058
512-367-5069
Mr. Fred Groff

Top of Texas Hunting
P.O. Box 30504
Amarillo TX
USA 79120
806-352-1106
Mr. G. Conner

Trans-Pecos Guide Service
P.O. Box 599
Sanderson TX
USA 79848
915-345-2629
Mr. G.W. Zachary

West Tex-New Mex Hunting
Services
P.O. Box 69
Ozona TX
USA 76943
915-392-2923
Mr. J. Rankin

Westminster Safaris Ltd.
3200 Louis Court, Ste. B
Plano TX
USA 75023
214-964-2213
Ms. J.A. Chaffee

Williamson, Col. Bill
Hunting Consultant
P.O. Box 27241
Austin TX
USA 78755
512-345-4891

Y.O. Ranch
Dept. SCI
Mountain Home TX
USA 78058
512-640-3222

Outfitters Directory: Hunting

North America

Young, Ron
6011 South Staples St.
Corpus Christi TX
USA 78413
512-993-1200

Utah

Adventure Unlimited
Box 27
Hurricane UT
USA 84737
801-635-2340
Mr. B. Branham

Diamond Ranch Outfitters
P.O. Box 209
Provo UT
USA 84603
801-377-3100
Mr. Wade Lemon

J.G. Guides & Outfitters
Dept. S.C.I., P.O. Box 41
Munroe UT
USA 84754
801-527-4107

Safron, Bob
USFS Federal Building
324 25th Street
Ogden UT
USA 84401

Sleeping Deer Outfitters Inc.
Box 1232
Kanarraville UT
USA 84742
801-586-9203
Mr. Scott Berry

Mexico

**Alcampo Hunting Adventures
Dr. Noriega Y
Garmandia 108
Hermosillo, Sonora
83000
Mexico
621-2-32-39
Telex: FLFFME 58669**

Big Game Outfitters
Sauzales No. 44
14330 Mexico, D. F.
Mexico
671-1177
671-2064
Mr. C.G. Hermosillo

Sonora Outfitting
Adolfo de la Huerta, #405
Colonia Pitic.
Hermosillo, Sonora
Mexico
011-52-621-48703

South America

Argentina

Safaris Del Neuquen
Gral. Roca 1028,
San Martin de los
Andes Prov de Neuquen
Argentina
944-7616

Brazil

Almeida, Antonio de
Caixa Postal 840 Sao Paulo
Brazil
227-0922
Mr. A. de Almeida

Notes

Outfitters Directory: Fishing

Australia

Nimrod Safaris
P.O. Box 472
Darwin
Australia 5794
089-81-1633
089-81-1256
Mr. B. Lees

Angus Corporation Limited
P.O. Box 30069
Lower Hutt
New Zealand
NZ-04-663-329

Simon Dickie Adventures Ltd.
P.O. Box sd682
Lake Tampo
New Zealand
74-89680

Westland Guiding Services
P.O. Box 38
Franz Josef Glacier
New Zealand
Ph 750 Telex thru 4349
Mr. B. Peterson

Lake Rotoroa Lodge
Nelson Lakes Ntl. Park
R.D. 3
Murchison South Island
New Zealand
64-54-69035
Mr. Bob Haswell

Danks New Zealand Safaris
and Tours
P.O. Box 8066
Kensington Whangarei
New Zealand
Mr. A.C. Wilson

North America

Canada East

New Brunswick

Fundy Lodge
P.O. Box
1856 Woodstock NB
Canada E0J 2B0
506-328-3571
506-755-2963

Hide Away Lodge
Box 820
Woodstock NB
Canada E0J 2B0
506-894-2413
506-328-2272
Carrie and Ivan Hayden

Nepisiquit River Camps
R.R. #5, Box 345
Bathurst NB
Canada E2A 3Y8
506-546-5873
Mr. Kenneth Gray

Wild Country
Wilderness Outfitters
P.O. Box 148
Plaster Rock NB
Canada E0J 1W0
506-356-2372
506-473-2907
Mr. J. Merritt

Newfoundland

Goose Bay Outfitters Ltd.
Sum: P.O. Box 171,
Happy Valley
Labrador
Canada A0P 1E0
709-896-2423
Win: 5 Lomac Rd.
St. John's, NFLD
Canada A1A 3M8
709-753-0550

Ontario

Colimar Lodge Ltd.
Route 2, Box 121
Jellicoe ONT
Canada P0T 1V0
807-879-2521
807-879-2565
Mr. Clayton Doucette

Elliot Lake Aviation
P.O. Box 425
Elliot Lake ONT
Canada P5A 2J8
705-848-7501

Fisherman's Wharf
Box 374
Meaford ONT
Canada N0H 1Y0
519-538-1390

Hales, Floyd
Fish Hunts
Beaverton ONT
Canada L0K 1A0
705-426-7415

Keyamawun Lodge
P.O. Box 303
Waterdown ONT
Canada L0R 2H0
416-689-4380
Mr. Stu Loten

Lift the Latch Lodge
French River
R.R. #2
Alban ONT
Canada P0M 1A0
705-857-2135 Summ
416-639-4570 Wint
Mr. Norm Beales

Northern Lights
Resort
Box 79A
Loring ONT
Canada
705-757-2554
Mr. H. Stroeher

Polar Bear Camp
and Fly-In Outfitters
22-5th Street,
P.O. Box 396
Cochrane ONT
Canada P0L 1C0
705-272-5890
705-272-4672
Mr. S. Konopelky

Red Pine Hunting
and Fishing Camp
1402 Altona Road
Pickering ONT
Canada L1V 1M1
416-286-2994

Outfitters Directory: Fishing

North America

The Dolphin Motel
549 Lakeshore Dr.
North Bay ONT
Canada P1A 2E5
705-472-5370

Waltonian Inn
R.R. #1
Callander ONT
Canada P0H 1H0
705-752-2060

Quebec

Cerf-Sau Inc.
Dept. G
40 Racine Street
Loretteville QUE
Canda G2B 1C6
418-843-0173
Mr. Gilles Shooner

Laurentian Ungava
Outfitters Ltd.
R.R. #7
Lachute QUE
Canada J8H 3W9
514-562-3832
Mr. J. Hume

Mistassini Lake
Outfitting Camps
Baie de Poste
Via Chibougamau QUE
Canada G0W 1C0
Mr. A. Matoosh

Montagnais Fishing and
Hunting Club
6357, Des Citelles
Orsainville QUE
Canada G1G 1E3
418-627-4165
418-585-2228
Mr. L. Valcourt

Normanic Inc.-Pourvoiries
Suite 103
2323, Boul. du Versant Nord
Sainte-Foy QUE
Canada G1N 4P4
418-681-1258
Mr. F. Lacombe

Square-Tail Lodge
P.O. Box 442
Morin Heights QUE
Canada J0R 1H0
514-226-3119
514-226-2049
Mr. & Mrs. Bob White

Toundratour Inc.
Chambeaux Club
319 East, St. Zotique
Montreal QUE
Canada H2S 1L5
514-270-7266
Mr. Henri Poupart

Tuktu Fishing & Hunting Club
Box 427
Ancienne-Lorette QUE
Canada G2E 4W6
418-872-3839

Canada North

Northwest Territories

Arctic Fishing Lodges
& Outfitters
Box 806
Yellowknife NWT
Canada X1A 2N6
403-873-4036
403-873-3626
Ms. Yvonne Quick

Guided Arctic
Expeditions
P.O. Box 2120
Inuvik NWT
Canada X0E 0T0
403-979-2408
Mr. T. Cook

True North Safaris
36 Morrison Drive
Yellowknife NWT
Canada X1A 1Z2
403-873-8533
Mr. G. Jaeb

Canada West

Alberta

Frontier Fishing Lodge
P.O. Box 4550
Edmonton AL
Canada T6E 5G4
403-433-4914 Wint
403-370-3501 Summ
Mr. J. Bricker

Great Bear (1986) Ltd.
Trophy Lodge
P.O. Box 36
Innisfail AL
Canada T0M 1A0
403-227-2907

Stricker's Outfitting Ltd.
Box 354
Wildwood AL
Canada T0E 2M0
403-325-3961

Timbermountain Packtrain
Box 511
Claresholm AL
Canada T0L 0T0
403-625-2931
Mr. D.D. Simpson

Trophy Hunting & Fishing
Consultants Ltd.
12 Cedardale Cr. S.W.
Calgary AL
Canada T2W 3Z5
403-251-3828
Mr. L.D. Biscope

British Columbia

Aurora Outfitters
Box 4150
Smithers BC
Canada V0J 2N0
604-847-4848
Mr. K. Oysmueller

Diamond M Outfitters Ltd.
P.O. Box 297
Atlin BC
Canada V0W 1A0
Radion Phone 2M8464
White Mtn. Channel
Mr. Jim Mattarozzo

Doern, Wally
566 Edkins Street
Quesnel BC
Canada V2J 1X9
604-992-2287

East Kootenay
Outfitters
14-21st Avenue S.
Cranrook BC
Canada V1C 3H1
604-426-2834
Mr. J. Juozaitis

Fawnie Mountain Outfitters
General Delivery
Anahim Lake BC
Canada V0L 1C0
Pr. George Radio Ph
H487487 Nimpo Chnl
Mr. John Blackwell

Outfitters Directory: Fishing

North America

Indian River Ranch
P.O. Box 360
Atlin BC
Canada V0W 1A0
Mr. D. Smith

Lamoureux Outfitters Ltd.
General Delivery
Ft. Ware BC
Canada V0J 3B0
Ft. Nelson Rodio Op
2M3827 Ft. Ware
Mr. M. Lamoureux

Moon Lake Outfitters Ltd.
P.O. Box 161
Atlin Bc
Canada V0W 1A0
604-651-7515
Mr. E. Smith

Moose Lake Lodge
General Delivery
Anahim Lake BC
Canada V0L 1C0
503-575-1152

Manitoba

Sickle Lake Lodge Ltd.
Box 364
Lynn Lake MAN
Canada R0B 0W0
204-356-2532 Summ
800-233-6846 Wint
Mr. Brian McIntosh

Saskatchewan

Misaw Lake Lodge
Box 1297
Unity SASK
Canada S0K 4L0
306-228-3828
Mr. Morice Miller

Wollaston Lake Lodge
General Delivery, Box G
Wollaston SASK
Canada S0J 3C0
306-633-2032 Summ
800-328-0628 Wint
Mr. & Mrs. Brian Elder

United States
North East

Iowa

Keeline, Jim H.
Registered Guide
Box 7044
Spirit Lake IA
USA 51360
712-336-5124
712-225-2168

Maine

Gentle Ben's Hunting
& Fising Lodge
Box 212 S1
Rockwood ME
USA 04478
207-534-2201
Mr. B. Pelletier

Pinkham's Fishing Lodge
P.O. Box M
Ashland ME
USA 04732
207-435-6954 US
506-753-3644 Can
Ms. Virginia Pinkham

The Bradford Camps, Inc.
RFD #1, Box 1125
Turner ME
USA 04282
207-225-3057 Wint
207-764-6112 Summ
Mr. Dave Youland

Whisperwood Lodge
& Cottages
North Belgrade ME
USA 04963
207-465-3983
Mr. & Mrs. A. Fitzgerald

Michigan

Big Sand Lake Lodge Ltd.
P.O. Box 646
Northville MI
USA 48167
313-420-4610
Ms. Liz McCarville

Waterbury Lake, Sask.
Munn & Associates
1409 Greenview Avenue
East Lansing MI
USA 48823
517-351-4080
Mr. John G. Munn

New York

Salmon River Outfitters
P.O. Box 117
Pulaski NY
USA 13142
315-298-5726
Captain Bill Brill

Shadow Charters
242 E. Main
Webster NY
USA 14580
716-265-3680
Mr. David DeVolder

Ohio

Grants Cabins
191 E. Washington Avenue
Marion OH
USA 43302
614-387-5571

Pennsylvania

Jim MacCarthy Adventures
4906 Creek Drive
Harrisburg PA
USA 17112
717-652-4374
717-545-1952

World Hunts Inc.
P.O. Box 777
Latrobe PA
USA 15650
412-537-7668
1-800-4-Hunting

United States
North West

Alaska

Alaska River Safaris Ltd.
4909 Rollins
Anchorage AK
USA 99508
907-333-2860
Mr. Ron Hyde

Brightwater Alaska
P.O. Box 110796-G
Anchorage AK
USA 99511
907-243-1922
Mr. Chuck Ash

Outfitters Directory: Fishing

North America

Bristol Bay Lodge
P.O. Box 6349
Anchorage AK
USA 99519
907-238-1714
Mr. & Mrs. Ron McMillian

Dodge Outfitters
SR Box 8800
Kodiak AK
USA 99615

Fishing Unlimited Lodges
P.O. Box 6301
Anchorage AK
USA 99502
907-243-5899
907-781-2213
Mr. K. Owsichek

Golden Horn Lodge
P.O. Box 6748
Anchorage AK
USA 99502
907-243-1455

Greatland Fish Company
P.O. Box 1935,
Eastchester Stn.
Anchorage AK
USA 99520
907-835-2310

Katmai Guide Service
Box 313
King Salmon AK
USA 99613
907-246-3030
Mr. J. Klutsch

Keeline, Jim
P.O. Box 1333
Juneau AK
USA 99801
712-336-5124
712-225-2168

Lamoureux, Gus & Frenchy
P.O. Box 4-444-S
Anchorage AK
USA 99509
907-248-4971
907-248-3012

Lazer, David L.
Master Guide
SRA Box 6877
Palmer AK
USA 99645
907-745-4504

Ole Creek Lodge
506 Ketchikan Street
Fairbanks AK
USA 99701
907-452-2421
Mr. & Mrs. Donald Haugen

Peninsula Outfitters and
Air Taxi
P.O. Box 1444
Kenai AK
USA 99611
907-776-5578

Ptarmigan Lake Lodge
1001 Lake View Terrace
Fairbanks AK
USA 99701
907-456-6967
Mr. U. Rahoi

Rocky Point Resort
P.O. Box 1251-FH
Petersburg AK
USA 99833
907-772-4420

Talaheim Lodge
4505 Spenard Road, #205
Anchorage AK
USA 99517
907-733-2815
Mr. Mark Miller

Tikchik Narrows Lodge
P.O. Box 220248
Anchorage AK
USA 99522
907-243-8450
Mr. Bud Hodson

Tim Hiner Professional
Fishing
P.O. Box 2122
Soldotna AK
USA 99669
907-262-9729

Unalakleet River Lodge
For reservations (Oct.-May):
Lynn and Penny Castle
P.O. Box 536
Bandera, Texas 78003
512-796-4909
Seasonal address
(June-Sept.):
Unalakleet River Lodge
P.O. Box 99
Unalakleet, Alaska 99684
907-624-3030

Whalers Cove Lodge
Killisnoo Harbor
Box 101
Angoon AK
USA 99820
907-788-3123
Mr. Richard Powers

Idaho

Aggipah River Trips
P.O. Box 425
Salmon ID
USA 83467
208-756-4167
Mr. Bill Bernt

Allison Ranch
7259 Cascade Drive
Boise ID
USA 83704
208-376-5270
Mr. Harold Thomas

Anderson Outfitting
4990 Valenty Road
Pocatello ID
USA 83202
208-237-6544
208-237-2664
Mr. Rbt. R. Anderson

Arctic Creek Lodge
P.O. Box 1166
North Fork ID
USA 83466
208-865-2166
Mr. Jack P. Smith

Barker River Trips
2124 Grelle
Lewiston ID
USA 83501
208-743-7459
Mr. J. Barker

Bay Area (Mother Bear)
Charters
Box 459
Bayview ID
USA 83803
208-683-2093
Ms. Sandra Morris

Beamer's Heller Bar
Box 1223
Lewiston ID
USA 83501
208-743-4800
Ms. M. Beamer

Outfitters Directory: Fishing

North America

Bear River Outfitters
Star Route 1, Box 1450
Montpelier ID
USA 83254
208-847-0263
Mr. M. Jensen

Bighorn Outfitters
Box 66
Carmen ID
USA 83462
208-756-3407
Mr. M. McFarland

Boulder Creek Outfitters
Incorporated
Box 119
Peck ID
USA 83545
208-486-6232
208-839-2282
Mr. T. Craig

Butler, Bruce
Box 478
Hailey Id
USA 83333
208-788-2468

Canyons Inc.
Box 823
McCall ID
USA 83638
208-634-4303
Les and Susan Bechdel

Castle Creek Outfitters
Box 2008
Salmon ID
USA 83467
208-344-6600
Mr. D. McAfee

Chamberlain Basin
Outfitters
Route 1, Box 240-A
Salmon ID
USA 83467
208-756-3715

Chilly Ranch
Star Route
Mackay ID
USA 83251
208-588-2584
Mr. M. Butler

Clearwater Outfitters
4088 Canyon Creek Road
Orofino ID
USA 83544
208-476-5971
Mr. L. Crane

Cross Outfitters
310 South 3rd East
Preston ID
USA 83263
208-852-1038
Mr. L.W. Cross

Custom River Tours
Box 7071
Biose ID
USA 83707
208-343-3343
Mr. K. Masoner

Diamond D Ranch Inc.
Box 1
Clayton ID
USA 83227
313-773-5850
Mr. T. Demorest

Dixie Outfitters Inc.
Box 33
Dixie ID
USA 83525
208-842-2417
Mr. W.E. Smith

Drury, Omer
Box 248
Troy ID
USA 83871
208-835-2126

Eakin Ridge Outfitters Inc.
Box 1382
Salmon ID
USA 83467
208-756-2047
Mr. Lamont Anderson

Epley's Idaho Outdoor
Adventure
Box 987
McCall ID
USA 83638
208-634-5173

Farbo, Thomas P.
Box 1297, 105 Adams Court
Orofino ID
USA 83544
208-476-4829

Flying Resort Ranches Inc.
Box 770
Salmon ID
USA 83467
208-756-6295
Mr. W.R. Guth

Gillihan's Guide Service
850 Jackson Ave.
Emmett ID
USA 83617
208-365-2750
Mr. Bob Gillihan

Happy Hollow Camps
Star Route Box 14
Salmon ID
USA 83467
208-756-3954
Mr. Martin Capps

Harrah's Middle Fork Lodge
3815 Rickenbacker
Boise ID
USA 83705
208-342-7888
208-342-7941
Mr. Nick Stuparich

Henry's Fork Anglers Inc.
Star Route, Last Chance
Ashton ID
USA 83420
208-558-7525
Mr. Michael J. Lawson

High Adventure River
Tours Inc.
Box 222
Twin Falls ID
USA 83303
208-733-0123
Mr. Randy McBride

Holiday River Expeditions
of Idaho
Route 2, Box 755
Grangeville ID
USA 83530
208-983-1518
Mr. Harold Stewart

Huehes River Expeditions
Box 217
Cambridge ID
USA 83610
208-257-3477
Mr. Jerry Hughes

Hussey, Rick (Ma) Selway
Lodge
Star Route, Iron Creek
Salmon ID
USA 83467
208-894-2451

Outfitters Directory: Fishing

North America

Idaho Adventures Inc.
Box 834
Salmon ID
USA 83467
208-756-2986
Mr. Hank Miller

Idaho Afloat
Box 542
Grangeville ID
USA 83530
208-983-2414
Mr. Scott Fasken

Idaho Big Game, Inc.
P.O. Box 2501
Salmon ID
USA 83467
208-756-4407
Mr. Jon Goodman

Idaho Guide Service Inc.
Box 1230
Sun Valley ID
USA 83353
208-726-3358
Mr. Olin Gardner

Idaho Wilderness Camps
Box 1516
Salmon ID
USA 83467
208-756-2850
Mr. Garry Merritt

Indian Creek Ranch
Route 2, Box 105
North Fork ID
USA 83466
Salmon Operator
Ask For 24F211
Mr. Jack W. Briggs

Juniper Mountain Outfitters
Route 3, Box 50
Caldwell ID
USA 83605
208-454-1172
Mr. S. Meholchick

Keating, Earl R. Jr.
Box 3
Gibbonsville ID
USA 83463
208-865-2252

Little Wood River Outfitters
Box 425
Carey ID
USA 83320
208-823-4414
Mr. Robert Hennefer

Lochsa River Outfitters
HC 75, Box 98
Kooskia ID
USA 83539
208p926-4149
Mr. Jack Nygaard

Lost Lake Outfitters
HCR 66, Box 226
Kooskia ID
USA 83539
208-926-4988
Mr. A. Latch

Lower Salmon Express Inc.
Box 1763
Lewiston ID
USA 83501
208-743-4404
504-758-0345
Mr. K. Jacks

MacKay Bar
3190 Airport Way
Boise ID
USA 83705
800-635-5336
208-344-1881
Mr. R. Eardley

Masoner's Whitewater
Adventures
Box 184
Twin Falls ID
USA 83301
208-733-4548
Mr. Elwood Masoner

McCarthy Outfitters
1127 S. Roosevelt
St. Boise ID
USA 83705
208-342-4231
Mr. Mike McCarthy

Meadow Creek Outfitters
Route 2, Box 264
Kooskia ID
USA 83530
208-9264759
Ms. Cheryl Bransford

Merritt's Saddlery
P.O. Box 1516
Salmon ID
USA 83467
208-756-4170
Mr. Garry Merritt

Middle Fork Rapid Transit
160 2nd Street West
Twin Falls ID
USA 83301
208-734-7890
Greg Edson and Bob Porter

Middle Fork River
Expeditions
P.O. Box 199
Stanley ID
USA 83278
208-774-3659 Summ
206-324-0364 Wint
Patrick and Jean Ridle

Middle Fork River Company
(The River Company)
Box 233
Sun Valley ID
USA 83353
208-726-8888
Mr. Steve Lentz

Middle Fork River Tours
Box 2368
Ketchum ID
USA 83340
208-774-2263
208-726-5666
Mr. Phil B. Crabtree

Moose Creek Outfitters
Box 1181
Orofino ID
USA 83544
208-476-5227
Mr. Richard Norris

Moyie River Outfitters
(Sweet's Guide Service)
HCR 85 Box 54
Bonners Ferry ID
USA 83805
208-267-2108
Mr. Stanley A. Sweet

Mystic Saddle Ranch
Box 0
Stanley ID
USA 83340
208-774-3591
Mr. Jeff Bitton

Norman Guth Inc.
Box D
Salmon ID
USA 83467
208-756-3279

Outfitters Directory: Fishing

North America

Northwest River
Expeditions Inc.
Box 824
North Fork ID
USA 83566
208-865-2534
Mr. Ed Link

Northwest River Company
Box 403
Boise ID
USA 83701
208-344-7119
Mr. Doug Tims

Paradise Outfitters
HCR 11, Box 74
Kamiah ID
USA 83536
208-935-0859
Mr. Rich Armiger

Pioneer Mountain Outfitters
Route 2, Box 5476
Twin Falls ID
USA 83301
208-734-3679
Mr. Thomas Proctor

Piquet, Laren
Route 2, Box 1205
Driggs ID
USA 83422
208-354-2786

Potts, Stanley
Outfitter
Box 1122
Hailey ID
USA 83333
208-788-4584

Priest Lake Guide Service
Star Route, Box 134
Nordman ID
USA 83848
208-443-2357
Ms. Jane E. Mehs

R & R Outdoors, Inc.
2755 Aspen Cove
Meridian ID
USA 83642
208-888-4676
Mr. Robert D. Black

Red River Corrals
Star Route, Box 18
Elk City ID
USA 83525
208-842-2228
Mr. A. George

Red Woods Outfitter
HC 2, Box 580
Pollock ID
USA 83547
208-628-3673
Mr. N.F. Woods

Renshaw, Jim
Star Route, Box 115
Kooskia ID
USA 83539
208-935-2829

Revell Enterprises
Box 674
Soda Springs ID
USA 83276
208-574-3016
Mr. P.K. Revell

River Adventures, Ltd.
Box 518
Riggins ID
USA 83549
208-628-3754
208-628-3952
Mr. M. Hinkley

River Odysseys
West (Row)
P.O. Box 579
Coeur d'Alene ID
USA 83814
208-765-0841
Mr. Peter Grubb

Rivers Navigation
Box 1223
Lewiston ID
USA 83501
208-743-4800
Mr. W. Beamer

Robson, Dale R.
Box 44
Felt ID
USA 83424
208-456-2861

Rocky Mountain River Tours
P.O. Box 2552
Boise ID
USA 83701
208-344-6668
208-756-4808
Mr. D. Mills

Ron's Flying Service
P.O. Box 401
Emmett ID
USA 83617
208-365-4946
Mr. R.K. Vaughn

Rusty Gore's Salmon River
Jet Boat and Float Trips
Box 806
North Fork ID
USA 83466
208-865-2371
208-756-6281
Mr. Russell Gore

S & S Outfitters
912 Burrell
Lewiston ID
USA 83501
208-746-3569
Mr. David Bream

Salmon Meadows Lodge
HC 75, Box 3410
New Meadows ID
USA 83654
208-347-2357
Mr. J.R. Thrash

Salmon River Boat Tours
Incorporated
Box 1185
North Fork ID
USA 83466
208-865-2512
Mr. Bob Smith

Salmon River Challenge
Incorporated
Box 1299
Riggins ID
USA 83549
208-628-3264
Mr. Pat Marek

Salmon River Lodge Inc.
Box 348
Jerome ID
USA 83338
208-324-3553
Mr. David Giles

Salmon River Whitewater
Incorporated
Box 1170, Hwy. 93 N.
Salmon ID
USA 83467
208-756-4452
800-545-3337
Mr. Steve Settles

Sawtooth Wilderness
Outfitters and Guides
730 W. Greenhurst
Nampa ID
USA 83651
208-466-8323
Mr. Leo V. Jarvis

Reader Service Card

Forward this form directly to advertiser. See directory for address.

I saw your advertisement in the Hunters' Guide.

I would like:

☐ Additional Information

☐ A List of References

☐ A Booking Form

☐ _____

My Name _____

Address _____

City _____

State/Prov. _____ Zip/Code _____

Country _____

Forward this form directly to advertiser. See directory for address.

I saw your advertisement in the Hunters' Guide.

I would like:

☐ Additional Information

☐ A List of References

☐ A Booking Form

☐ _____

My Name _____

Address _____

City _____

State/Prov. _____ Zip/Code _____

Country _____

Forward this form directly to advertiser. See directory for address.

I saw your advertisement in the Hunters' Guide.

I would like:

☐ Additional Information

☐ A List of References

☐ A Booking Form

☐ _____

My Name _____

Address _____

City _____

State/Prov. _____ Zip/Code _____

Country _____

How to Order: Fill in the order blank on this page and mail to Hunters Guide.

Phone Orders: To process your order faster call us at (902) 468-2365 between 9 a.m. and 5 p.m. (EST) Monday through Friday. Please have your MasterCard, American Express or Visa number ready.

Payment: In order to keep the price of merchandise as low as possible, payment must accompany all orders. Send check, money order, Visa, American Express or MasterCard number with expiration date. Please do NOT send cash. All prices are quoted in U.S. funds.

Back Orders: Although sufficient inventories are on hand, occasionally unanticipated demand can reduce stocks rapidly. Should it become necessary to back order any items, we will contact you and give you an expected shipping date.

Merchandise Returns: We will be happy to accept the return of any item in its original condition purchased, for exchange or refund up to three weeks from the original date of shipment.

Please Allow 2 to 4 Weeks for Delivery.

Qty		Name of Item				Item Price	Total Price
		Outhouse Book				12.95	
		The North Book				30.00	
		Hunters Guide 88				25.00	
		Canadian Nature Diary 88				12.95	
	M	The Ultimate Vest	☐ Brown	☐ Blue	☐ Camouflage	125.00	
	L	The Ultimate Vest	☐ Brown	☐ Blue	☐ Camouflage	125.00	

☐ Check here to receive the Hunters Guide every year.   **TOTAL**

U.S. FUNDS

ORDERED BY:

Name _____

Address _____

City _____ State _____ Zip _____

Please charge my: ☐ MasterCard   ☐ VISA   ☐ American Express   ☐ I've enclosed a ☐ money order   ☐ cheque.

Card # _____ Daytime Phone _____

SHIP TO:

Name _____

Address _____

City _____ State _____ Zip _____

NO COD ORDERS. Please do not send cash through the mail.
Mail to: Hunters Guide, 25 MacDonald Ave., Dartmouth, N.S., Canada B3B 1C6.

Qty		Name of Item				Item Price	Total Price
		Outhouse Book				12.95	
		The North Book				30.00	
		Hunters Guide 88				25.00	
		Canadian Nature Diary 88				12.95	
	M	The Ultimate Vest	☐ Brown	☐ Blue	☐ Camouflage	125.00	
	L	The Ultimate Vest	☐ Brown	☐ Blue	☐ Camouflage	125.00	

☐ Check here to receive the Hunters Guide every year.   **TOTAL**

U.S. FUNDS

ORDERED BY:

Name _____

Address _____

City _____ State _____ Zip _____

Please charge my: ☐ MasterCard   ☐ VISA   ☐ American Express   ☐ I've enclosed a ☐ money order   ☐ cheque.

Card # _____ Daytime Phone _____

SHIP TO:

Name _____

Address _____

City _____ State _____ Zip _____

NO COD ORDERS. Please do not send cash through the mail.
Mail to: Hunters Guide, 25 MacDonald Ave., Dartmouth, N.S., Canada B3B 1C6.

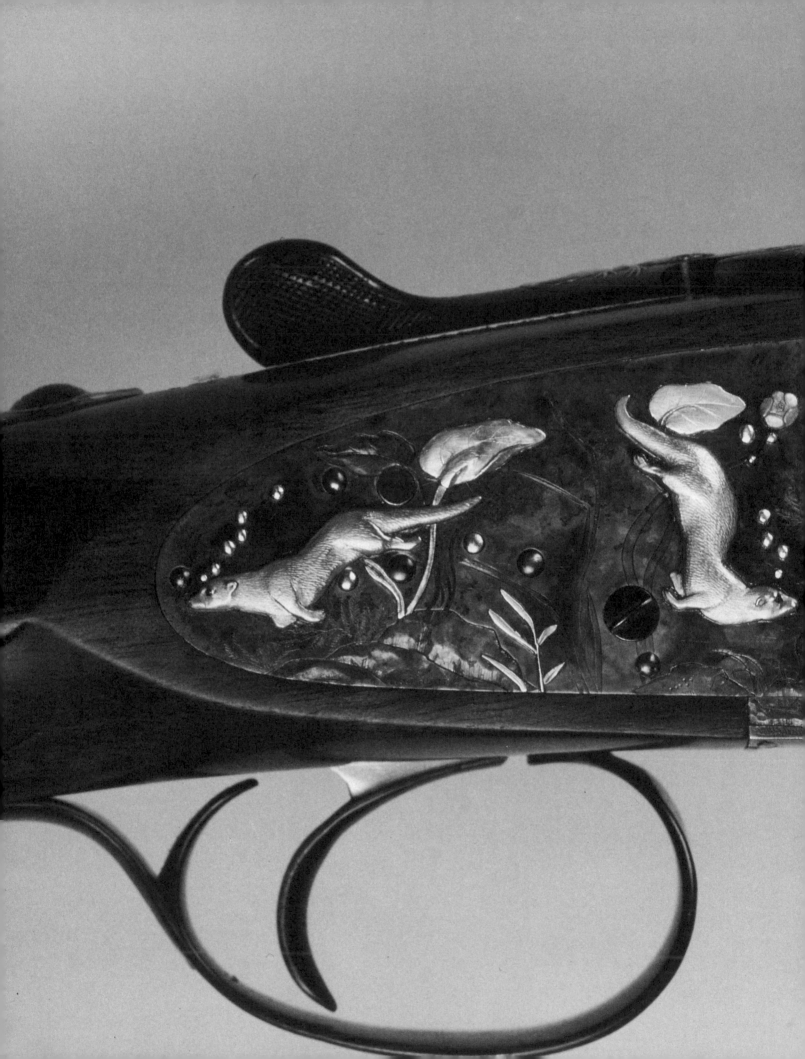